NAPOLEON BLACK

THE CRUCIFIED LIFE

Embracing the Cross in a Self-Indulgent Age

FOREWORD BY TEDDY JONES

Extra MILE Innovators
Kingston, Jamaica WI

COPYRIGHT

Published by
Extra MILE Innovators
54 Montgomery Avenue,
Kingston 10, Jamaica W.I.
www.extramileja.com
ruthtaylor@extramileja.com
Tele: (1876) 782-9893

Cover, Layout, and eBook by
N.D. Author Services [NDAS]
www.NDAuthorServices.com

DEDICATION

To Rev. Courtney Richards

ENDORSEMENTS

The cross dealt once and for all with our guilt and shame, but —wonder of wonders—it seems like twenty-first century Christianity is ashamed of the cross. Yet it stands forever as the greatest worship experience this world has *never* seen! In three hours of darkness the glory of God shone brightly like never before, and the wo/man who embraces it will live forever more!

Pastor Black has done us a tremendous favour by inviting us to join a Turkish born sinner-turned-saint in celebrating the rallying point of true liberation: *"But God forbid that I should glory, save in the cross of our Lord Jesus Christ, by whom the world is crucified unto me, and I unto the world."*

—Delano Palmer,
Former Deputy President,
Jamaica Theological Seminary

.   .   .   .   .

It seems as if Christianity has become a fad rather than a lifestyle lived through the direction of the Spirit. This timely volume *The Crucified Life* is well needed and provides the reader with matters for serious consideration and reflection. It speaks to the heart of what Christianity is about, death to self and yieldedness to the Holy Spirit. It makes the bold statement, and I agree, about the surrender of self. It reads:

...the surrender of the self to the glory of God for the lib-eration, empowerment and the uplift of others. Those who are not willing to offer this level of surrender cannot be His and do not know Him, no matter what else they may profess.

It also speaks to the goal of Christianity, Christlikeness. It is a must-read for those who want to be godly and model the virtues of our God.

—Dr. Carlton Dennis,
Former President,
Associated Gospel Assemblies

FOREWORD

This notion of every day being a bed of roses is a myth. It is in the crucible of life that legacy is minted...

Faith in the crucible is required for joy there and in the place of milk and honey...

Life's seemingly random chaotic debilitating negative events like getting a call and coming home to see your house on fire with all your belongings up in smoke pull on your inner strength. They beg questions that can fling a big man to the ground writhing in agony. They assault nice sounding religious phrases. When they fling us into the crucible it is at that point that one's concept of God has to be more than just a theory, more than just the Pastor's words. Faith has to become yours... your personal and deeply help conviction that in the midst of the chaos there is still a divine plan at work...

It is in the crucible that the mettle of faith is tested. I observed...as I stood there... No Counseling Theories and Techniques 101 would suffice... Through it all they smiled. They could laugh. Now it's my time to speak with a theology of praxis... to help them through the matters arising when the smoke no longer rises...

In the crucible, the pain was not mitigated but in the earthquake busted sepulchre the joy was unbridled. The paradox of life is the juxtaposition of both in an inextricably bound knot of experience...

All of the above contain the word 'crucible,' which my wife thinks is one of my favourite words. She is probably right. In fact, all of the above are directly taken from Facebook posts that I have made over the last 10 years. Crucible arises from the same root word as crucifixion. Similarly the word excruciating, which literally means out of the cross. You can understand therefore, why this sampling of statements from me with the word crucible now forms part of the foreword for *The Crucified Life.*

The author is so close to me that I will only refrain from copying the phrase "closer than a brother" out of reverential awe of Jesus. Our friendship is sealed by the very cross of Jesus because it is the model of the cross defined love of Jesus which guides our friendship. To say, then that it is an honour to write the foreword for this book would do grave injustice, but you get the point (I hope).

There is something to be said about one being able to write from one's head, and yet another to be able to write from one's heart. This book was written from Napoleon's heart and his head. It represents his critical reflections upon his lived experience, and his deep passion to follow and model his Lord, to the fullest extent. Yes including embracing suffering.

Recently a Youth Ministry that I had already admired rose much higher in my esteem as they spoke with me about the concept behind the 2019 staging of their annual Youth Conference. The ethos of it was to help Christians to suffer well. I shared the concept as my Whatsapp status and the first response, which was almost immediate, was laced with incredulity. Others quickly rubbished the very thought. None of this surprised me. Not when we have a massive, well oiled machinery pumping into our veins the mantra that it is unbiblical and even sinful for Christians to suffer.

The predominant theology, if it can be called that, of suffering is that it is incompatible with being a successful child of God. Into that milieu, Napoleon proposes the crucified life, not as an option but as core, as part of the course, as the life to which we are called. If there was ever a book that the term "cutting against the grain" fits it is this one.

Rev. Black takes us through the events of that day with a meticulousness reminiscent of Dr. Luke, the Gospel writer. His description of the flogging forced my mind back to Mel Gibson's "Passion of The Christ" for a mental picture. We naturally revolt against this but it is what it is. It is what happened that day. To seek to escape the Scriptural teachings on suffering, which are unmistakable in the cross is to be the proverbial ostrich with its head buried in the sand.

Never mind the glitz and the glamour, the jets and the Bentleys which the pulpit hawkers parade as the outstretched sceptre of the genie in a bottle kind of God who superintends over a factory of idols. This is the contrast of the lived experience of the masses of faithful brothers and sisters in the so called "Third World," and that of those within walking distance of the palatial residences of the seed collectors in the so called "First World." Then there is the seemingly paradoxical news of Missionaries on the brink of death because they can't afford medication on the missions stipend.

These are the ethical dilemmas of those who desire to obey their Lord but live in the midst of a people of unclean hands, and traverse pass the distribution of the spoils of scamming without holding out their hand for their share. These stories from the crucible can only make sense because there is indeed and in fact such a thing as the crucified life, and that life provides effervescence, power, resilience, and a push back that enables the one who lives that life to say "no." Buoyed by the knowledge that God is able to deliver them from hell's wrath, but IF NOT they will not capitulate to the immoral juggernauts because they have already died and neither evil nor death has any hold over them.

The way up is down. May we descend into our greatness as we embrace and live the crucified life. Onwards and forward, it's YHWH's will.

—Rev. Teddy Jones
Author and Chairman of the
Missionary Church Association in Jamaica

PREFACE

This very brief work represents some very basic thoughts in an area of Christian life which is fundamental. When we accept Jesus Christ as Lord and Saviour we assume that with it would come all the 'benefits of His passion.' But it seems that not much of the benefits of sharing in His suffering are generally mentioned. And yet, this was a part of Paul's cry, that he might know Jesus and share the fellowship of His suffering.

I hope that this work will challenge each of us to evaluate how we understand living for Jesus. The times are urgent and I think that in this season of so much ease, luxury and complacency, we need to remind ourselves that at the heart of Christianity is the cross of Jesus Christ.

And while the cross is the symbol of Christian triumph and victory, it is also the embodiment of that oxymoron that Jesus left us—life is not to be found in holding on to living in the self, but in the willingness to dying to the self.

In His death, He taught us so much about what it means to live. When He surrendered Himself to death, He did it knowing full well the agony that He would face in going to crucifixion. And yet in the moment of the deepest crisis of His life, He was able to tell His Father that His will was what He had come to fulfil.

His death on the cross epitomises the surrender of the self to God and speaks volumes to us in how we may live and how we may find lasting victory. It is in suffering that we find the essence of the strength, the grace and the beauty of the Lord.

My prayer is particularly for those who have struggled long and hard, who have prayed for healing and deliverance and have found none. It is that such persons will embrace the miracle of the grace of God when the pain remains after praying, and God replies that His grace is sufficient. May the crucified life bring you peace with God as in stillness you find His heart for your life.

—Napoleon Black, 2019

ACKNOWLEDGEMENTS

I am taking tales out of school here. A group of us used to meet once per month under the discipleship care of Rev. Courtney Richards of RENEWED Ministries. On this particular occasion, most of us found ourselves distressed about how difficult things have been with us in ministry. Some of us who have families reported the trauma that our wives were undergoing; others talked about how difficult ministry was and just finding their place.

We were all but giving up because the expectations that we had—expectations of God's miraculous intervention, expectations of the ready acceptance of our ministry and our families by others, expectations that we would meet least-resistance were just not happening.

Courtney listened to us all this while. Then came the bombshell. He simply told us that we have it all wrong. The miraculous may happen in that way, but equally miraculous and spectacular is when God takes us through pain, when it seems that none of the traditional expectations are coming to pass. "The miracle," he told us, "lies in our embracing God in pain, that we might discover Him. It is He who changes things and people. We are only vessels of that process." He frightened us further. "The things we seek, the changes, the acceptance etc, might take years and some of us might never see the changes. You are only a line in the story."

A line in the story? I left thinking, "years … years of pain." But I also knew he was right. I had a better view of God and the Christian journey and I think that TJ, Omar, Robert and Richard left with a better sense too. So I dedicate this work to

Courtney, a great man of God. He models the crucified life better than anyone else that I know.

I thank my children Jameil and Yanique and my wife Aneita for walking with me on this journey of the crucified life.

I also give thanks to God for the privilege of putting this work together. It has been an honour. A special thanks to Ruth Taylor for the great work she did in helping me to work through this material to make it more presentable. Thanks too, to my home assembly, Maverley Gospel Hall for your support and the continued privilege of serving.

Thank you too, for choosing to read this work. I hope that you might find something in it that will help you understand better the call to the crucified life.

INTRODUCTION

For a convicted felon standing before a magistrate in the time when Rome ruled the world, the most frightful words to hear coming from the mouth of the magistrate would be, "I hereby sentence you to be crucified!" Crucifixion was a most excruciating and sordid affair. Death could not come quickly enough. Indeed, the Romans would not allow their citizens, no matter how heinous their crime, to face that kind of capital punishment. It was only reserved for non-Roman citizens.

The New Testament pounces on the idea of crucifixion as the essence of Christianity. The cross is its central symbol and the Man hanging there the only means to truth and life. The cross then remains crucial to the life of the believer without which the faith becomes meaningless, hollow and vain.

This work then comes out of a desire to see more closely, what the scriptures require of those of us called to be Christians who must live their lives, as Jesus commands, taking up the cross and following Him daily. Since it deals with the cross, it becomes an appeal to examine again the call to daily pain, daily struggle and the daily facing of death. It is a call to return to the essence of true discipling and discipleship—the taking up of the cross and following Jesus.

Living by way of the cross and its implications seem lost on the significant portion of modern Christianity. This is not by way of judgment, but rather a hope that we will return to the basic message of the cross. This seems to be more honored in the breach than in the rule in a time when notions of self-control, sacrifice, humility and meekness are being jettisoned in favour of an easy theology of personal security found in self-help at its worst or at best God helping those who help themselves.

The first section of this work invites a reflection on the cross and the significance of the cross and our response to it. The second section of this work offers a closer look at some of the factors preventing the cross walk and how best to deal with them, that we might in effect die to live. The third section takes the form of a practical forty day devotional walk taking the time to solidify the major principles of this work.

It is expected that this work will help to give a clear presentation of the discipleship that the Bible and Jesus call us to. It is expected that readers will learn to appreciate some of the finer details of Christian living that sometimes are glossed over in favour of the undoubted benefits of living for Jesus. It is expected as well that through this work individuals and communities may be brought to some greater level of trans-formation towards Christlikeness.

TABLE OF CONTENTS

PART 1:
THE CRUCIFIXION AND SUFFERING

1.

WHAT HAPPENED THAT DAY

...they crucified Him (Matthew 15:35)

In 1968, a team of archaeologists exploring some cave-tombs in northern Israel found in them fifteen ossuaries containing the bones of thirty five individuals. These boxes and their contents dated back to just about the time of Jesus. Among the remains in one of those limestone urns was discovered the bones of a man, probably about thirty years old, who had been crucified.

Those who examined the remains found what appeared to be a hole in his right forearm which was probably the result of brutal contact between a nail and the bone of the forearm. Holes were also observed in the man's heels. It appeared though that these nails ran through the side of the heel into the wood, not as customarily thought with both feet together with one in front of the other. On further examination, it was also observed that this man's legs were also fractured. For the first time, modern light was thrown on what was undoubtedly the horrifying ordeal of Roman crucifixion.

Crucifixion was a popular form of capital punishment in ancient times. The Egyptians, Greeks, Assyrians and Persians all practised it. Some have pointed to Deuteronomy 21:22, 23 (cf. Galatians 3:13) as making the case that the Jews also practised crucifixion.

Probably the most well-known case of mass crucifixion was the case of the 6000 followers of Spartacus who led a revolt against Rome in about 70BC. These were crucified along the roadway between Capua and Rome as a ghastly reminder to would-be revolutionaries.

By the time of Jesus, crucifixion was reserved by the ruling Romans for criminals of the worst kind. It is believed that Rome took the practice of crucifixion from the Carthaginians. Crucifixion was so humiliating an ordeal that no Roman citizen would be allowed to be crucified. Except for high treason, the worst that could happen to a Roman Citizen was that he would have been sent somewhere in exile. Roman soldiers often amused themselves by crucifying civilians from other nations.

Before crucifixion, the convict was stripped of all his clothes. Nothing was left. He would then be whipped with a specially designed strap made with the expressed intention of battering blood vessels, tearing flesh and cutting through skin.

After this beating, if he were still able to stand—many died from the beating alone—he would be required to take upon his battered shoulders the horizontal piece of what was to be his cross to the place of crucifixion. There he would be nailed to the cross, hands and feet and left to die.

For some, death came quickly, but for most the cross was an appalling and lingering horror. Nailed to the cross, the convict found breathing extremely difficult. He could inhale readily, but exhaling was torture. To exhale, he would have to try to lift his torso by pushing against his feet nailed to the cross. The very thought of pushing against the nails with the feet to bring the body up to exhale was itself agony. Further, the weight of the body was difficult to manage. The body was in an unnatural position, legs slightly bent to accommodate the heels struck through together by the nail. The arms were not tightly drawn, but given some leverage which allowed for lifting the body if there was strength to do it. But every attempt at trying to raise or to adjust the body was terribly painful. On the cross, the convict had the sense of every bone being out of joint.

After a while, as the victim hung there, there would be feelings of physical shock, if not from the previous beating, certainly from being nailed to the cross. He would begin to feel very thirsty, to struggle with dehydration and eventually exhaustion. Every time he tried to pull himself up to inhale his whole frame would tremble under the pressure, and since the lungs could not readily release the air trapped there, it began to expand more and more. Most died of asphyxiation.

Some would be given cheap liquor to face the pain. Pain and stupor would be better than pain alone. At death, the victim's mangled body would be left on the cross for vultures to eat. There was no greater ignominy.

THE MOST FAMOUS EVENT IN HISTORY

There can be no doubt that Jesus' crucifixion is the most famous in all of history. As He walked about in His ministry, He would have witnessed scenes of men with their crosses going to be crucified. Indeed, He referred to the very thing as a symbol of true discipleship (Matthew 16:24; Mark 8:34, 10:21; Luke 9:23). He knew too that His day would soon come.

Finally, from the Biblical texts, He set His face resolutely towards Jerusalem, for He knew that He too had to face crucifixion (Luke 9:51). While this action did not lead Him directly to His death, it set the stage and the context which highlighted His ultimate purpose in coming to earth—to do the will of the Father, by dying on the cross.

The closing scenes of Jesus' life probably began with His institution of the sign of the New Covenant at Passover- the Breaking of the Bread. God is a God of Covenants. And most covenants were sealed with some sign or means of memorialising the agreement. For instance, the Covenant with Noah was sealed with the sign of the rainbow, the covenant with Abraham was sealed with circumcision, the covenant with Moses was sealed with the Sabbath Day regulation and the sign of the New Covenant, Jesus says, was to be the taking of the bread and the cup, symbolising, and memorialising His death.

From there, that evening, Jesus went to the Mount of Olives where He travailed at the burden He would carry upon the cross. He was in so much grief and agony that His sweat became as great drops of blood. By this time, Judas had agreed to betray Jesus by standing in court as a witness against Him. Soon he appeared with temple guards to arrest Jesus. According to John, a fracas developed and in the mêlée Peter almost killed Malchus, the servant of the High Priest, ending up cutting off Malchus's ear. Jesus healed the servant—His final miracle before His resurrection. The texts do not say if Jesus was harmed in this incident. But He was bound and taken to the Sanhedrin.

At the time of Jesus and under Roman occupation, The Sanhedrin was the officially recognised legal and political representatives of the people of Israel to their Roman overlords. The Sanhedrin was made up of seventy one married men, thirty years and older who had a good grasp of the Jewish Law. It was comprised of a High Priest, twenty four Pharisees, twenty four Sadducees, and twenty two scribes.

On the night of Jesus' arrest Jesus was first tried by Annas, the retired High priest and later that night by Caiaphas, the then current high priest and son-in-law of Annas.

But this trial was a mockery and a dreadful travesty of justice. According to the tradition of the Elders, criminal trials could not be held after dark, or before the morning sacrifice, and further, the trial was to take place in a public place. All of these were violated.

Also, the traditions did not allow for an accused man to accuse himself, but in the absence of Judas, there was none to accuse Jesus. Additionally, where there are witnesses, they had to agree in every detail. The trumped-up witnesses failed here again as the Sanhedrin's star witness realised that he could not go through with what he had initially agreed to.

And what was more, according to the traditions, to show deference and disinterest, there had to be a twenty-four hour period between the trial and the verdict and a further three days between the verdict and the sentencing. But here none of these rules were observed.

To give the appearance of credibility and legitimacy to the travesty of that night, the following morning, Jesus was given a "public" trial before the Sanhedrin. There He was also "found guilty."

After the mockery of the Sanhedrin episodes, Jesus was taken before Pilate. Pilate was the Roman Governor and was himself under suspicion by Rome for treachery. The cards were all but stacked against him in this plot of intrigue. Five times he tried to set Jesus free, but the Priests would have none of it. He told the Jews that he found no fault with Him. Jesus was innocent.

When he learnt that Jesus was from Galilee he sent Jesus over to Herod. Herod was unimpressed with Jesus, since Jesus refused to perform any miracles for him. He dismissively had Jesus sent back to Pilate.

Pilate thought he was playing the game well. But his gamble did not pay off; he lost, even though he gained the friendship of his long-time enemy, Herod.

With Jesus back on his hands, he was now at a loss. He tried another strategy. He offered a choice between Jesus, the healer, and Barabbas the insurrectionist and murderer; again he lost for he was still left with Jesus. The crowd roared its dis- approval and required of Pilate, Barabbas—a terrorist of sorts.

To show his "fairness" he ordered Jesus to be whipped. Jesus was taken by a centurion and a squad of soldiers and was beaten mercilessly.

It is generally thought that Jesus received the thirty nine lashes prescribed in Jewish traditions, but this is not necessar- ily the case as the Roman soldiers had no obligation to regard Jewish observances on this account. This flogging was a thing for Roman soldiers to perform and to get their kicks from.

So, they took off Jesus' clothes, leaving nothing on, tied Him up and began what for them was a sordid sport. Among the weapon they used was a short strap made of strips of leather. Pieces of sharp metal or glass were tied to the end of this strap along with small metal balls.

They began across His back, then down to the legs and then into the head. As the beating continued, the flesh would begin to give way under the pressure. Flesh would begin to tear and blood began to seep out. When there was no place left on His back to beat, the soldiers would then turn Him over and beat Him across His belly, His chest and His face. Roman soldiers were efficient in everything they did. They could beat a man, bringing him to as near to death as possible without killing him, even though some died from the ordeal.

By this time, Jesus would have been in great pain from the beating, and by the time they loosed Him from the whipping post, some of His flesh probably would be loosely hanging down His back. Small pieces would be seen on the ground around. For most, it would have been a sickening sight.

After the flogging, Pilate had Jesus brought back out to the crowd dressed in the scarlet robe the soldiers had thrown over Him. While Jesus was away being beaten, the Pharisees seemed to organise a change in strategy.

Now the gauntlet was thrown down to Pilate. If he let Jesus go, then he was not Caesar's friend. A political storm was brewing and Pilate took the bait. His political career was on the line. Before Rome's representative, the charge against Jesus changed. It was now that Jesus claimed to be a king, a rival to Roman rule and Roman interest in Israel.

His attempt to please the people on all counts failed. And his attempts to set Jesus free failed. His question betrayed his frustration "Then what should I do with Jesus?" The crowd roared, "Crucify Him!"

Pilate took water and washed his hands. This was so strange, since only he could have given the command to crucify anyone. Even though the Romans turned a blind eye to mob justice, as in the case of the murder of Stephen, and the attempted murder of the woman caught in adultery, crucifixion had to be ordered by Rome. He told the Jews to see to it themselves.

At the command to crucify Jesus, the scene changed forever. The soldiers took Jesus and continued the mockery homage festival. The whole company of soldiers were now around Jesus, mocking Him, jeering Him. Since the charge against Him was the claim that He was king of the Jews, the soldiers mock-ingly plaited a rough crown made of a prickly tree and rammed it into Jesus' skull. The effect of this would be to heighten the pain in Jesus' head. Doctors say that the cranium is saturated with nerve endings and thorns stuck in these nerve endings would heighten Jesus torture to all but unbear-able proportions. Not only that, but, the blood running down into His battered face and particularly into His eyes must have created additional distress for Him. On top of that, they took the "sceptre" they had given Him and beat Him in His head with it—the head already bearing the crown of thorns.

When the mock festivities were over and they were satisfied, they prepared Him to take the horizontal beam of what would be His cross. Jesus probably would be in severe shock by now.

They then gave Jesus the cross-beam to walk the six hundred or so yards to the place of His crucifixion. Someone walked be-fore the procession with the written charge against Him. As He went along the raw flesh would rub against the wood He car-ried adding more pressure to His pain. Every step of the way, everything was done to intensify the agony and pain of Jesus, but it was important that He should not die on the way; the command from Pilate was that He should be crucified.

As Jesus walked along, His body gave way under the weight of the cross beam. The soldiers must have been in a rage. They grabbed a man and ordered him to carry the beam. Jesus was to arrive at Golgotha alive. The command had to be carried out as given.

When they got to the place of crucifixion, the soldiers took the cross- beam from Simon of North Africa. They nailed the cross beam to the groove in the top of the vertical piece that was already there and made a T. About the middle of the T was a small piece of board on which some condemned persons could rest their buttocks.

They then placed the T cross on the ground. They then took Jesus and laid Him on the ground astride the cross. They took one of His arms and stretched it. Not all the way. It was to have some leverage. The soldier would then feel for the sink at the wrist and pound a nail through the hand into the wood. What was the "nail" was really a seven or eight inch spike. He would do the same with the other. The pain was excruciating. And bear in mind that the term "excruciate" comes from the Latin which means "out of the cross."

They then held Jesus' feet; put them, the one on top of the other. The soldier would drive the nail through the ankle out through the heel into the wood, fastening Him there. He was now pinned to the wood.

When the soldiers were sure that He was properly secure, they would hoist Him and secure the cross into place. At that, Jesus' weight would come tumbling down against His aching hands. He would try to brace His feet back to bear the weight, but every shift or movement was agony.

Jesus was on the cross from nine o' clock that morning to about three that afternoon. As He hung there, some of the people would hurl insults at Him. Others mourned over Him.

Soon He was dead. Some have wondered why Jesus died so quickly. When the news was reported to Pilate, even he was surprised that Jesus was already dead. But bear in mind that Jesus was up from the day before the crucifixion. He went through three Jewish trials that night—Annas, Caiaphas, and the public trial. He also went through trial before Pilate, then taken across to Herod, then back to Pilate, all in one night. He would have been tired, drained, dragged around, beaten and insulted.

He was crushed by the Jews, spat on, boxed and generally humiliated. He was beaten by the Romans, taunted and tortured by them. He was then beaten for crucifixion. No ordinary human being could have withstood so much. But Jesus did.

As evening approached, particularly in respect to the Jewish Sabbath, the soldiers sought to do what they usually would do —break the feet of the convicts to hasten their deaths. They broke the feet of the two men crucified with Jesus, but when they came to Jesus, they found that He was already dead.

But just to make sure, the soldier ran his sword through Jesus' rib cage into His heart. Blood and water came gushing out. Jesus was truly crucified.

FROM THE GARDEN TO THE TOMB

A Possible Chronology of Jesus' Last Day

When we pull together all that we know from the Gospels, the events from Gethsemane to Golgotha may have been as follows:

1. *Gethsemane* (Matthew 26:36–56; Mark 14:32–51; Luke 22:39–53; John 18: 1–11)

2. *The Prayer Travail* (Matthew 26:36–46; Mark 14:32–42, Lu. 22:39–46).

Jesus normally comes to Gethsemane to pray (Luke 22:39, Jn. 18:2). This evening, after having had the Last Passover Meal and instituting the Covenant Sign Supper, He takes His disciples with Him to Gethsemane. The word Gethsemane means "oil press" probably named for the many olive trees there. It may also be significant in that He too was about to be "pressed."

A number of things happen here:

- He separates Peter, James and John to be nearer to Him than the other disciples as He prays.
- He goes a distance away from them and begins to pray.
- Jesus asks His Father to consider the possibility of another way, while surrendering His will to the Father's will.
- During this first episode, an angel appears and strengthens Him.

- He continues to pray until His sweat becomes as drops of blood.
- After this first prayer appeal, He returns to the three to find them sleeping.
- Evidently, this first prayer ordeal lasted for over an hour as He asked Peter if he could not stay up for even an hour suggesting that an hour was a short time at prayer.
- He returns to His second prayer episode with the same prayer request. This time He is more resolute in embracing the Father's will that He should drink the cup.
- He returns to the disciples to find them still sleeping.
- He goes back a third time to pray as He did before.
- After the third time, He comes back and finds them still sleeping, and Judas turns up.

3. *The Arrest* (Mark 14:32–42; Luke 22:47–53; John 18:1–11)

- Judas leads a party of soldiers, (probably temple soldiers) and some officials from the Chief Priests and Pharisees
- Jesus asks them who they are looking for
- They reply that they are looking for Jesus
- Jesus identifies Himself
- The arresting party falls to the ground
- He again asks them who they are looking for
- Again they reply that they are looking for Jesus
- Judas now embraces Jesus and kisses Him, to confirm to the soldiers that it was Jesus
- Jesus asks Judas if that is how he is betraying Him.
- Jesus then appeals to them to take Him and let the disciples go
- As they tried to arrest Jesus, a fracas developed in which Peter cuts off the high priest's servant, Malchus' ear.

- Jesus restores the ear and orders Peter to put away the sword, reminding him that He had to drink the cup that His Father had given Him to drink. He also upbraids the detachment for coming to take Him so cowardly.
- They seize Him and take Him away

4. *Jesus Before Jewish Officialdom* (Matthew 26:57–68; Mark 14:53–65; Luke 22:63–65; John 18:12–24)

- It was probably late night by now. Jesus was taken before the Jews before He was taken before the Romans.

Before Annas

- He was taken to the house of the former High Priest, Annas, and it seems here that this part of His trial was totally without warrant. Annas would have had no right to have Jesus appear before him.
- The examination begins:
    Annas begins by questioning Jesus about His ministry and about His disciples Jesus tells them that what He did and who He was with over the period is public knowledge, so they should go and ask those. At this one of the council members hit Jesus across His face, accusing Jesus of being disrespectful to the High Priest. Jesus insists that He had done nothing wrong. Annas then sends Him to Caiaphas the then current High Priest.

Before Caiaphas

- It is at this meeting that the full Sanhedrin met to examine Jesus. Evidently, by now, Judas, their star witness had changed his mind and decided not to go through with the plan to stand as a witness against Jesus. This seemed to have thrown the prosecution into turmoil.

- Many persons came forward and told lies about Jesus. These lies could not stand.
- Eventually, they found two who said that He said that He was able to destroy the Temple and rebuild it in three days. Even on that the testimonies did not agree. For a sentence to be binding the testimony of he witnesses had to agree in every detail.
- The priest asked Jesus to answer to the charge, but He did not say anything.
- The Priest then used the legal form of address to which Jesus was obliged to answer by saying—I charge you under oath by the living God... Jesus was thus obliged to answer. He answered affirming that He was the Christ, the Son of God
- The priest tore his clothes at this, something he was not allowed to do (Leviticus 10:6, 21:10). He said that what Jesus said was blasphemy.
- He consulted with the Sanhedrin which concluded that Jesus was worthy of death.
- At this they blindfolded Him, began to spit in His face, hit Him with their fists and slap Him and taunt and insult Him, commanding Him to reveal who hit Him.
- After this, the temple guards took Him and beat Him.
- It was during this ordeal at Caiaphas' house that Peter denied Him three times.
- By now it was early morning and realising what he had done Judas took back the money he had gotten from the priest, they would not accept it. He threw the money on the ground and went out and hanged himself.

5. *The Public Trial* (Luke 22:66)

After the trial at Annas's house and the trial at Caiaphas's house, Luke seems to record a third public trial.
Probably, this trial was to help to give legitimacy to
their actions of the night before, because according to
Jewish Law, trial could not take place at night. So this
day break trial was evidently to give legitimacy to what
was done the night before.

The Sanhedrin again met and Jesus was placed before them. The issue here seemed to establish in the
hearing of all, Jesus confirming that He was the Christ.

In this trial, Jesus again confirms to them that He is
the Son of God. They were satisfied. They did not need
any other witness.

6. *Jesus Before Roman Officialdom* (John 18:28–19:16; Luke
   23:1–25; Mark 15:1–20; Matthew 27:11–26)
   Pilate felt bothered by the Jews in them bringing Jesus to him, so early in the morning. He told them to deal
   with the matter according to their law. But the Jews
   would have none of it, they wanted death by crucifixion. They told Pilate that they had no right to execute
   anyone.

   • Jesus is called into a private interview with Pilate.
   • Pilate gets flustered at Jesus' attitude and responses
     or lack thereof.
   • After the private interview he took Jesus out and told
     the waiting Jesus that he found no basis for charging
     Him with any crime.
   • The Jews then argue that Jesus is a trouble maker be-
     cause He stirs up people with His teachings that He
     started in Galilee and had now come to Jerusalem.
   • When Pilate learns that Jesus was from Galilee, he
     had Him sent to Herod who was in Jerusalem at the
     time.
   • They took Jesus over to Herod.

- Herod was not impressed with Jesus since He would not perform a miracle, nor would He answer his questions.
- Herod and his soldiers ridiculed Jesus and also had a mock homage celebration for Him, dressing Him in an elegant robe.
- Herod had Him sent back to Pilate and since then Pilate and Herod, sworn enemies, became friends
- Pilate called the Jewish leaders together and told them that neither he nor Herod had found any reason for Jesus to die.
- He knew that it was out of envy that they Jews had brought Jesus to him.
- He told them that as was customary at Passover he was willing to release a prisoner, only this time it was a choice between Jesus and the notorious in-surrectionist and murderer, Barabbas.
- Pilate takes his seat on the official Judgment Seat, the Gabbatha, as called by the Jews.
- His wife sends him a message to say that he should have nothing to do with Jesus, because she was very disturbed in her sleep concerning Him.
- The people shouted for the release of Barabbas
- Pilate had Jesus flogged. This probably was the worst of the flogging that Jesus faced and it would have been here that He was flogged in the way a con-demned man was flogged.
- Then there was the second mock homage paid to Je-sus by the Roman guards. This time they plaited a crown of thorns and pushed it into His skull. They put a purple robe on Him and paid mock homage to Him. They also beat Him in His head.
- After the beating and the mocking, Pilate goes out to the Jews, explaining to them that Jesus was innocent. He found no fault in Him.

- He then brings Jesus out wearing the clothes of His mock trial, saying, "*Ecce Homo*—behold the man!"
- At this the people began to demand that Jesus be crucified
- Pilate told them to do it themselves for he found no basis for doing it.
- The Jews insisted that according to their Law, Jesus had to die because He was guilty of blasphemy
- Pilate became afraid and took Jesus back inside, trying to talk to Him. Jesus would not answer, except to say that Pilate had no power over Him, except power given by His Father.
- From then on Pilate tried to free Jesus.
- In the attempt to free Jesus, the people told him that if he freed Jesus, then he was no friend of Caesar, insisting that anyone who claimed to be a king opposed Caesar.
- Pilate finally relented. He again took his official seat at the Gabbatha to pass judgement on Jesus
- He offered Jesus back to the Jews as their King
- They refused Him clamouring that Jesus should be crucified and that they have no king but Caesar.
- Pilate then washed his hands in front of them and handed Jesus over to be crucified.
- He told them that the matter was their responsibility. The people said that the blood of Jesus would be upon them and their children.
- The soldiers then prepared Him for crucifixion with the continuation of the mock homage, including the beating.

7. *Via Dolorosa* (Latin for *Way of Grief* or *Way of Suffering*) (Luke 23:26-32)
   After the beating and the mocking Jesus is then given His cross to carry to the place of crucifixion, in this case, to Golgotha. The soldiers would guide Jesus to the place.

Jesus takes His cross and begins the journey to the place of crucifixion. But because of the beating, He could not carry it any further and so, they ordered Simon of Cyrene to take it behind Jesus.

Along the way were some women who wailed at His end. Jesus tells them not to wail for Him, but for themselves and for their children and that it will be better for those who have no children.

When they took Him to Golgotha, they gave Him some mixture of wine and gall to drink, but when He tasted it, He would not drink it.

Then they crucified Him there.

2.

THE SURRENDERED LIFE

Come down from the cross and save yourself! (Mark 15:30)

There was a kind of pathos that accompanied Jesus' hanging there on the cross. While He lived, He had done so much; He had exhibited so much power. He had spoken so strongly, inveighing against wrong, injustice and immorality. He came across as invincible. He had described Himself in terms equal to deity.

But here He was now. The system had gotten Him. They had waited for this moment and now they had Him. He was now totally in their control. He was now nailed to a cross, saying that He was thirsty, committing the care of His mother to one of His disciples. He was asking why His God had forsaken Him. There seemed to be a sad and almost paradoxical end to a life lived with so much fire, energy and vitality. The sarcasm and cynicism of sections of the crowd was rife with theatre-like amusement.

DEATH BY THE CROSS

But the crowd missed the point entirely, for Jesus was born to go to the cross. He was born for that purpose. The essence of His humanity is to be summed up in that one thought—He came to be crucified. This crucifixion was not an end in itself, but it served as the end of that which had to end.

The fact of human rebellion against God was to be consumed in the cross. The curse of sin, the imprisonment by the Law (Galatians 3:23, 24) and the hopelessness of human futility were all to be consumed there. This cross answered so much of who we are as human beings—our struggles, our failures, our anxieties. The cross serves as the end of humanity turned in on itself and offers for the first time, in full view, the possibility of new things.

It was there, at the cross, that Jesus gave a troubled man hope. It was there that He wiped out the sin of those who nailed Him to the tree and in perfect tranquillity He declared His work finished, and then He dismissed His spirit.

For Jesus, crucifixion was not so much the fact of death, but more importantly the means of death. Jesus came not just to die but to die by crucifixion—God's appointed way. It was God's will that He should suffer, to be crushed and to be made a guilt offering (Isaiah 53:10). It was the 'thorning' of the head, the piercing of the hands and feet with hammer and nails, the giving of the back to the strap and the opening of the heart to the sword, all these answer every ailment of the human condition, whether wounded by abrasions, lacerations, puncturing, or by avulsions.

So Jesus did not only surrender Himself to death, but He surrendered Himself to a particular means by which He would die, the means that was most horrid and barbarous, the means that was most cruel in all of human history—death by crucifixion, for sin is not only horrible, it is absolutely horrible. It affected every part of the body, no part is left untouched by its ravaging force.

It was "the fullness of time" as Paul describes it (Galatians 4:4)—a time filled with this dreadful evil, called crucifixion, a time when Roman rule was unparalleled in the then known world and which would bequeath to the world an ugly godless order, a time that at last, brought all the major civilizations of the world together in one place. The charge that hung over Jesus' head was written in three languages we are told—the language of religion, the language of politics and the language of fine culture (John 19:20).

Jesus was born to face a particular kind of death. Several attempts were made to kill Him. Herod sought to murder Him in infancy (Matthew. 2:7-18) and the Jews tried to push Him over a precipice (Luke 4:28-30). Neither means was God's appointed.

He was born to be crucified and He knew it. It was the most painful means. He did not see Himself as being tortured to death. He saw Himself bringing glory to the name of His Father through His death. He speaks most movingly of His death in John 12:20-34. It is there He tells some Greek visitors that He would die by being lifted up. In verses 27 and 28, He speaks of the trouble in His heart, but confidently affirmed that it was for the glorifying of His Father through His death on the cross that He had come.

LEAVING OURSELVES AT THE CROSS

Finding life through the cross is the way for us as Christians too. The call to live as a Christian begins there—at the cross, the place of death. And while we may have our various formulae for how one becomes a Christian, the proof of the Christ-life lies not so much in the confession nor in the creed, but critically in the letting go of everything and dying at the cross.

Before we encounter the resurrected life of God, we must leave ourselves at the cross. Jesus modelled it perfectly here. He was helplessly thirsty (John 19:38) and no doubt as He hung there He would have been tempted to use His powers to quench His thirst—just as He was tempted to use His powers to turn stone into bread (Luke 4:3).

He knew that upon the cross He had to endure this thirst. It is easy to want to try to meet the needs of our bodies in our way, as quickly as we can, especially if we feel that nothing is particularly wrong with the way we propose to meet the need. But that was not open to Jesus as He hung there. He could not meet the most basic need of His body for Himself—the need for water.

For us, we begin our encounter with God at that place too, a hunger and thirst for God. The beatitude says it well. Blessed are those who hunger and thirst for righteousness, for they will be filled (Matthew 5:6)

This hunger and thirst is the hunger for God which must mark those who desire God—to be free, to be different, to be truly spiritual, to be god-like, god-centred and godly. Hunger and thirst is the admission of a deep dissatisfaction of the soul which must mark the crucified life. It is not possible to be filled with the Holy Spirit until there is this acknowledgement and self-emptying. Too often believers expect the fullness of God's Spirit while still filled with all kinds of ideas, attitudes, emotions, thoughts and conduct which run contrary to the will of God.

The crucified life demands the silencing of the soul in a cry of thirst for God. It is the acknowledgement that the natural will not and cannot do, and only God will suffice. It is the putting away of the thirst for that which does not satisfy, to craving a thirst for that which is truly life-giving and which truly satisfies. It is out of the belly of such that streams of living waters will flow.

Jacob had that sort of experience in his encounter with God in Genesis 32. The text begins in darkness (22) and ends in light (31). Jacob begins the encounter with the name Jacob (27) and ends it with the name Israel (28). Jacob was willing to risk his all his possessions so that he could encounter God. He started in fear and ended in hope. But all this was because he was prepared to pay the price—fighting with God all night, willing to be hit in the hip for his trouble, walking with the pain of a limp for the rest of his life, all because he wanted God and the blessing of God.

Sometimes as believers we expect a shortcut to the blessing of renewal, but for most of us, the blessing only comes when God sees in us the passion and the tenacity to have what we request of Him. Jacob was willing to pay the price for that renewal. He paid it and he was renewed.

A second observation from the cross is this: From there, Jesus cast His eyes down to His mother (John 19:26, 27). He knew her pain, but He did not take it away from her. He watched her watching Him, watching her bearing her pain. But He did not stop the pain that she was feeling. Probably in her own mind came scenes of how He had stopped the pain of so many—the widow at Nain, for instance, where He brought back her dead son to life may have come to her mind (Luke 7:11-17)

And here again, He used nothing in Himself to prevent or even to appease the pain of His mother, even if she wished it. His mother was very important to Him, but there was little that Jesus did to take away His mother's pain. He watched her, stoically, as she watched Him die—naked and bleeding upon the cross. He felt her humiliation at what they had done to Him, but He did not soothe away her hurt.

He had told the women of Jerusalem not to weep for Him (Luke 23:28). In the Nain episode, His heart went out to the widowed woman on her way to bury her son. He gave the widow her son again. He had no such word for His mother. He would not come down from the cross and go to His mother. At best he could only place His mother under the care of another.

This is the nature of the crucified life, for in crucifixion, the will of God is more important, much more important that the pain of the sense of loss of a mother as precious as that must be. The Nazarite was not allowed to defile himself with the body of the dead, even if it were the body of a mother or a father, a sister or a brother (Numbers 6:7) even though a priest could (Ezekiel 44:25). This Nazarite vow was the symbol of the extremity of true discipleship.

And already, Jesus had spoken of discipleship as forsaking all for the will of God (Luke 14:26). He had invited young man to follow Him, but the young man had told Him that he was willing to follow, but first he would have to bury his father (Luke 9:58-60).

There can be no mistake about it, the crucified life demands leaving loved ones behind as precious as they are and going on to the place of solitary confinement. Death is that 'solitary confinement'-a place of aloneness till new life miraculously sprouts out of that which is planted.

The crucified life forges a scrutiny and a surrender of all relationships such that the examination will reveal that no relationship, no desire take place over the pursuit of God. All such, remains or becomes idolatry and adultery.

And in those dark hours when Jesus, quite literally, faced hell, He felt so alone. The confinement to the solitary place is the discipline of discovering the joys of the crucified life. The sins of the world were being heaped upon Him and He felt abandoned by His Father.

It is the reverse of what was described above. With His mother, He had to give her up, in a manner of speaking, but here, He felt given up. It is like the farmer releasing the seed to the ground and covering it over with the soil. Feel with Jesus as He sensed Himself falling away from his Father's hand to be locked away in the cold, damp, dark earth.

Again, there was nothing He could do and for the first time we see in Jesus something we had not seen before, because He had never had to bear this before. He asked His Father, "... why... (Mark 15:34)?" This question was not one born out of ignorance, nor was it out of anxious fright, but in the cut and thrust of the crucified life, the answers we know and the confidence we have are not enough, and so our answers and confidence must come from another place. The question was heard on high, but the will of the Father had to be done and Jesus knew it.

His concerns were deep and real—His painful thirst, His separation from His mother and now His separation from His heavenly Father. But He knew that the cross was an important part of His surrendering to the will of His Father. The writer of the Hebrews describes it as Jesus learning obedience (Hebrews 5:8). Surrender means pain and in the Christian sense, a pain which takes us to the end of ourselves, reviews our relationship with others and assesses our knowledge and assumptions about God. The cross we embrace means nothing, if first it does not take us to the end of ourselves.

Being planted by God can be very debilitating. That for most of us is a very difficult experience. It is here that we ask the hardest questions of ourselves and of God. Why have you forsaken me? Why can't I hear you? Where are you when it hurts so badly?

It is important to remember that there can be no oak of righteousness unless there is a planting of the Lord (Isaiah 61:3). There can be no tree bearing fruit unless there is the planting by the river (Psalm 1:3). Planting is not an end in itself and sometimes in the gloom, sightlessness and depth of our crucifixion we tend to lose our sense of who we are. Faith demands that exchange. We move from knowledge of ourselves to knowledge of what God sees in and of us.

But that is only a part of the story, because pain tends to cause us to turn in on ourselves. The lessons of the cross teach us otherwise. The cross must point us to others. In Jesus' case, in His pain, He was able to reach out to one of the men who, not long before, was cursing Him and hurling insults at Him (Mark 15:32), but who somehow came to his senses and asked Him for life, real life. Jesus told him that he would be with Him in paradise (Luke 23:39-43).

The crucified life demands the same of us. It demands that on the individual plain, those who may need our greatest attention are those who call for our attention, not in pleasantries shared or expressed, but in the insults they first start hurling at us.

The attraction to such lies in their unattractiveness to us, which first hides their hurt, their loneliness, their anger and the longings in their hearts hidden by their joining in to attack and insult and ridicule us.

The crucified life demands ignoring that insult to reach into the space of that individual and offering him hope. The best words he heard were the last words he probably heard —"today, you will be with me in paradise."

But Jesus goes further than the individual level. The individual level of the offer lies in the fact that it was requested, but what happens when nothing is requested and there is an arrogant posturing? Jesus extended to the wild maddened bloodthirsty crowd a similar offer. In their frenzy they were in merriment that He was on the cross. And yet, He offered them forgiveness (Luke 23:34). They did not ask for it, but He extended it nonetheless.

They really did not know what they were doing. In their wild blindness they had demanded that He be crucified. Now, there He was upon the cross, and there He was, looking at them. He had a perspective of things that they did not have and so He poured out forgiveness upon them. They asked that He be crucified. He asked that they be forgiven.

So He deals with this man, and then He deals with the people—the one repenting from hostility and turning to Him and He forgives and frees him, the other even in their hostility He forgives them nonetheless. Paul sums it up aptly when he writes, "While we were still sinners He died for us" (Romans 5:8).

One of the best tests of our character lies in how we respond in our pain particularly to those who hurt us. The crucified life requires that those who hurt us, must be offered hope when they ask for it as in the case of the brother hanging on the cross, and it must be offered to those who continue to hurt us even when they seem joyfully gleeful at our painful condition. There is no other way.

But Jesus also talks to His Father. The Father who had forsaken Him, He now calls to Him to receive His spirit (Luke 24:46). His work was all but done. This was no semi-conscious babbling here. He was fully aware of what was happening to Him while He hung on the cross. Knowing that His Father would have done what He had asked, He pronounced His work finished (John 19:30) and then dismissed His spirit (John 19:30). The crucified life ends with the conscious and deliberate dismissal of the spirit.

There is no true spiritual life until there is spiritual surrender to the Giver of spiritual life. It is the risk of letting go of the security of self-knowledge, self-actualisation and self-guarantees to the embrace the childlike certainty of a God who keeps, in the face of death.

"Into your hands I surrender my spirit," must be the cry of every child of God who desires to be like God. The fashioning into Christlikeness begins with the surrender of the self—

body, soul and spirit—the conscious and the unconscious, the will—both voluntary and involuntary, the reflexive and the deliberate.

THE CROSS AS THE SYMBOL OF SURRENDER

The cross is above all else the symbol of surrender to find true life, but it also smells of death. The crucified life begins by seeing itself nailed to the cross. It means that while others seem at liberty to do as they please, the Christian is not, for something of himself is nailed there. It means that he can do little about his thirst. It means that while his mother's pain may be great, there is nothing he will do out of God's will for his life to stop her pain; it means that God seems to be bearing down on him instead of coming to his rescue—that is the essence of the crucified life. It is that place of learning that which is indis- pensable to growing. It is learnt best in the blessing of death by the cross, where head, hands, feet and heart are pierced, that self-blood may run out and that the body may be infused with the life of the Spirit.

So the crucified life is not the place of the glamour of mir- acles and the fulfilment of promises. It is not the place of nam- ing and claiming the rights and the riches of the kingdom. The crucified life is the place of the darkest part of night, it is the valley of the shadow of death, and it is the place of being broken and alone in the darkness of the belly of the earth.

For us as Christians, God calls us to surrender ourselves. We cannot live the Christian life with our will, with our emotions, with our intellect. The Christian life requires a full surrender of everything—all that we have and all that we are, to God. It can be no other way. It demands that we surrender everything to Jesus—our will, emotion, intellect and attitude. Everything must first go to the cross. Proverbs 3:5, 6 says, "Trust in the Lord with all your heart and lean not on your own under- standing; in all your ways acknowledge him, and he will make your paths straight."

This is a verse so easily quoted but so easily misunderstood. The straight paths of life come only after the surrender of self. It comes when the reliance for life and living shifts from mind, intellect and emotion. It does not require the denial of these capacities, but the surrender of them on and at the cross. Too often, we want to understand all that God is doing before we can obey Him. This is dangerous. He may opt to reveal His will if He pleases, but we are required to trust even when we don't understand.

Additionally, the scriptures also make it clear that spiritual things are spiritually understood (1 Corinthians 2:14). This means that it takes more than the natural application of the mind to really see and know the will and the purpose of God. That is why the mind has to be renewed and this is spiritual renewal. It is as we understand and respond by way of the Spirit that God is pleased with us. Crucifixion must however first take place before we can understand things from the Spirit's perspective.

One of the tragedies of the Christian life is that people and leaders in particular try to block, or to prevent the work of the Holy Spirit because they do not 'understand' what is happening. Some even go so far as to label it foolishness or worse, 'of the devil.' From the text above, it may be that the flesh is still standing in the way.

The un-renewed mind has caused many to miss what God does and how God acts. It was this sad state of affairs which led some Pharisees to accuse Jesus of being mad, of having a demon, of casting out demons by the power of the devil (John 10:20, Mark 3:22).

It was this same failure which led many to ridicule the events of Pentecost (Acts 2) because their understanding was in darkness (Eph. 4:18). To live the Christian life, we cannot seek in any way to save ourselves. We cannot save ourselves from the embarrassment of hanging there on the cross. We cannot save ourselves from the pain of our thirst and we cannot stop our blood from running out. We must not.

Jesus made some very important points on this. For instance He says, "if you want to keep your life, you will lose it (John 12:25)." It is as simple as that.

How then do we live the crucified life? It begins with understanding what Jesus requires. He says that the way for the tree to really grow is that first the seed dies in the earth. But significantly, as pointed out above, this seed is *planted*, not buried and we must strive to know the difference. There is no place for mourning loss, but rather for expecting the fulfilment of purpose.

It is the giving up of the self that we are born with. It is taking the old creation to the cross with all of its strengths, all of its weaknesses and all of its in-betweens.

Sometimes we give the impression that when people come to God, all they have to give up are their bad ways. But I have read somewhere that even our tears of repentance must be washed in the blood of the Lamb.

An important aspect that sometimes we fail to surrender at the cross is our personalities. We feel that our personality type ought to come across with us into the resurrected life, but that is not necessarily so. We must give up our personalities as well, so that we may be fully surrendered. Quite often hidden in our personalities are the very things that make sin attractive to us and us attractive and attracted to sin. It has often been said that we cannot do anything about our personalities. But surely, while we are fully nailed to the cross, God can take that too and teach us obedience.

Living the crucified life begins with understanding spiritual surrender of self. Most of us have lived our lives on self-interest and even now as believers in Jesus we still practice self-interest. Even the good things that we do for others, we do hoping that *we* would be better for doing it. Paul talks about it when he talks about being able to speak in tongues and to prophesy and to exercise the gift of faith without love. His point is that we may do all the seemingly spiritual things out of self-interest, and sometimes love and trust have nothing to do with the exercise of the gifts of the Spirit in us.

But the crucified life begins with trusting God who calls us to surrender. We all know that trust to a relationship is like breath to the body. The crucified life demands a trust of God that we have never exercised before. We must trust God to take us to the point of the death of ourselves. We must resist the temptation to resist Him and to resist what He is doing. There is something innate to us which causes us to resist the unknown. It is that self-preservation component which inheres in all of us because we assume that the unknown is risky and the risk may somehow create too many challenges for us.

But that is the very point that God calls us to when He calls us to crucifixion. We believe that a bird in the hand is worth two in the bush. We believe that it is better to stick with the evil that we know than to risk what we do not know. The self-life encourages us to stay within the boundaries and the securities of what we already know about ourselves and can deal with for ourselves.

Remember the story of the men on the boat during the storm (Luke 8:22). Jesus was asleep. A storm suddenly comes up as was customary on the Sea of Galilee. The men knew what they had to do, so they got ready and began to do it. They even woke Jesus. They responded to what they knew, for they were in crisis. They felt themselves to be in great danger.

How could they save themselves and trust themselves to a Jesus who was asleep in the face of the storm at the same time? But they obviously did not realise that Jesus needed no saving.

In Christian thinking, God does not gain our trust. We go to Him trusting Him one hundred percent. We tend to take the worldly concept of trust to our relationship with God and with others. Trust in Christian thinking begins with the full hundred. It begins with making the full investment. Until we begin to understand that we must trust God fully, then we will not begin to appreciate what it means to live the crucified life.

Sometimes, we take with us into the life we live, a broken or damaged concept of trust, because somewhere in the back of our minds we feel the need to hold back something.

Like Ananias and Sapphira we keep back something and often pretend that we have given everything. It is this pretence at giving everything that affronts the Spirit of God.

Or we feel that God is holding out on us. There is the constant danger of giving in to the first lie recorded in the Bible. Satan told Eve that God could not be trusted, that God was holding out on them. There is that subtle danger of believing just that.

The crucified life demands the surrender of everything—my personality, my character, my strengths, my weaknesses, my talents, my attitude, everything, so that there will not be any trace of the old life when the new life is poured out. We burst and are rendered useless when we try to pour the new wine into the old skins (Matthew 9:17).

Learning Obedience through Crucifixion

Secondly, the crucified life involves understanding what God wants to do in us through being crucified. As mentioned earlier, it is through crucifixion that Jesus learned obedience. It is a difficult thought to grasp. What is there that Jesus did not know and needed to learn? The heart of the point must be that we are to be committed to release everything to God no matter how painful it is, because the greater the pain, the more critical the lessons to be learnt and the greater the need for trust.

This is not masochism, for that would be self-serving. It is going through whatever difficulties we must so that Christ might be glorified in us. And Christ is glorified in us only as we obey Him. The greatest test of our obedience comes particularly in the attitude of our response to Him in the midst of pain. Yes, in the midst of His pain Jesus asked His Father the 'why' question. However, It was not a question about "why me?" but a question which really called on God for assurance of His presence.

The Christian must learn obedience and so it is at the cross that the hedge is often adjusted. The promises of God seem to be suspended, the blessings seem to be arrested and there is a sense that one has nothing to hold on to. It is the attitude of obedience which is important here. This is where many balk and falter, the lesson is not learned, obedience is compromised and sometimes the process has to start all over again.

Job knew this well. He was already living the crucified life. All that he was and all that he had already belonged to God. The devil accused and slandered him before God. "Job is serving you because of what he can get from you!" was the cruel accusation (Job 1:9-11).

God spoke up in Job's defence. "You are wrong about him. Take everything from him and you will see" (Job 1:12).

We see the epic story there as it unfolds. The story ends on the triumphant note that despite his hardships Job honoured the Lord. That kind of honouring of God can only come when the old life is crucified and things are held in their right perspective.

CRUCIFIED TO FIND LIFE

In the crucified life, we must understand the freedom to die. The cross is not an end in itself. Its goal is that through surrender, through death, there might be a new beginning. Crucifixion risks death so that one might be born anew and to live an empowered life, not now according to the former ways, but according to the new way, the way of the Spirit. I will say more about the new creation later on.

It is a surrender which makes it possible for Christ to live the resurrected life through us. We become dead and He lives in and through us. That is why Paul writes that it is He who both wills in us and does in us His good pleasure (Philippians 2:13). This is a most profound statement. The crucified life creates the context in which we might truly live. A man may not live in the Spirit until he is dead to the natural. This is what epitomises his humanity. In a true sense, the altar of death becomes the very place where God gives him life that he may be what God intended him to be in the first place, and it is there that the fullness of his humanity is most profoundly affirmed.

THE FALLEN SEED: A STUDY OF JOHN 12:20-34

Some Greek converts to Judaism had come up to Jerusalem to worship at the Feast. They asked Phillip, one of the disciples, if they could see Jesus. Philip tells Andrew and, as seems customary, Andrew tells Jesus. Jesus tells them that the time for Him to be glorified is at hand.

He analogises His impending death to the falling of a seed into the ground with the expressed purpose, not that it would die and remain dead, but that it would release its true potential in death by producing many seeds by its dying.

He explained further that the person who seeks to preserve his life from going to that point will in the end lose everything, including his own life as by his refusal to be planted, he proves that there is nothing in him to reproduce.

Notwithstanding that, Jesus reveals the anxiety He felt at dying. The anxiety may have tempted Him to seek to abort the mission. But He knew He could not, because it was for the very reason that He came.

Then there was the paternal affirmation by way of the voice from heaven. His Father speaks audibly not for Jesus' sake, but for the benefit of those around, even though some thought that the voice was in fact thunder.

Jesus was careful to keep the attention of those listening to Him very focussed. He explains that in His death the world was about to be judged and the ruler of the world, Satan, would be thrown out. His death would be by way of being lifted up, and by being lifted up, all men would be drawn to Him. John comments that in saying this, Jesus was indicating the type of death He would undergo.

Again, there was uncertainty in the minds of the hearers about who the Son of Man is. Jesus explains to them that they would have the light for a while longer and that in a little while, the light would be taken and darkness would overtake the people. He invited them to put their trust in the light while it was still with them, so that they might become the sons of light. After this he left and hid Himself from them.

From the text, there are a few points that may need special attention. The discussion in general sets Jesus out as the very source of light and life. He offered light and life in the prediction of His death.

Secondly, He saw His death as being 'glorified.' Significantly, in the fact of being lifted up in death, there comes that multiplied effect of the impartation of more life, something which would not have resulted had He not died.

Thirdly, He insists that whoever serves Him, must follow Him. Obviously this includes the willingness to impart life and light through a similar death—the surrender of the self to the glory of God for the liberation, empowerment and the uplift of others.

Those who are not willing to offer this level of surrender cannot be His and do not know Him, no matter what else they may profess.

The falling of the seed, then, plays a critical role in the crucified life. Without it, God cannot be glorified in the life of the individual. There is no doubt that it will cause anxiety, and being planted will create a deep sense of aloneness, loss and pain, but it is in that act of transformation or probably metamorphosis that the individual loses himself to find himself, not now in himself, but as given to the glory of God and the drawing of men to Jesus Christ.

Curiously, Jesus hides Himself from them. Death-talk of this sort tends to put people on edge. The message of the crucified life stands up against traditional notions, it shifts the balance away from what is tried and proven, what is known, what is safe, to a place of risk, to a place of moving beyond the limits of what is thought to be secure, to test the extent and the measure of one's trust in God in the way that nothing else does.

It forces one to listen again to the voice of the Spirit for sometimes arrogance stands in the way of the opportunity to find true life. Arrogance resists surrender. Arrogance stands in the way of true discipleship. Discipleship is marked by the humility. And humility always embraces faith in God. The greatest friend of the false life, the carnal life, the pre-crucified life, a life empty of the power of the Spirit, is arrogance.

Being challenged to die is always resisted. Who wants to die? Arrogance will have none of that. Like the Laodiceans, arrogance wants us to believe that we are well, that we are okay, that we are empowered just as we are.

A message calling for death, especially to the arrogant who might think that they are alive without encountering the crucified life, will bring offence and sometimes the messenger will have to hide himself for a season.

3.

THE POWER OF SUFFERING

For it has been granted to you on behalf of Christ not only to believe on Him, but also to suffer for him... (Philippians 1:30)

S uffering has always been an important theme in the life of the Christian. It is critical that we grasp it that we might appreciate its place. So the scriptures say:

- Now if we are children, then we are heirs—heirs of God and co-heirs with Christ if indeed we share in his sufferings, in order that we may also share in his glory (Romans 8:17)
- In fact, everyone who wants to live a godly life in Christ Jesus will be persecuted (2 Timothy 3:12)
- However, if you suffer as a Christian do not be ashamed but praise God that you bear the name (1 Peter 4:16)

An important aspect, indeed foundational to the teaching of the apostles, was the teaching across the early church of the place of suffering. In Acts 14:21-22, the message of the kingdom is couched in the language of suffering, "Then they returned to Lystra, Iconium and Antioch, strengthening the disciples and encouraging them to remain true to the faith. 'We must go through many hardships to enter the kingdom of God,'" they said.

This was not a statement for those who were being challenged to become Christians, but was for those who had already placed their faith in Jesus as Saviour and Lord. This was a statement made to the disciples to *encourage* them and to *strengthen* their faith!

The inevitability of suffering in the faith is identified in Paul's comments in Romans 5:8 and 12:12. In these texts, he highlights the consequences of suffering for the believer and the attitude that the believer ought to have in the face of suffering.

He argues that the believer should face suffering with joyful resolve because "we know that suffering produces perseverance; perseverance, character; and character, hope.'"

This is one of Paul's 'we know' statements that cannot be grasped merely intellectually. To the natural mind, suffering balks at God's fairness, His care and His justice and His general interest in our wellbeing, but for Paul, there was knowledge from another place. We know that suffering is not an end in itself, but it produces the virtue of character which pleases God.

Note the progression which is so often missed—suffering produces, perseverance, perseverance produces character and character produces hope. Sometimes we presume to offer hope without character and to form character without perseverance and the cornerstone of perseverance is our response to suffering.

Again, this is not the suffering of being a busy-body as Peter points out, but the suffering and wounding that comes as a necessary consequence of a God-honouring life.

THE PROSPERITY DOCTRINE AND SUFFERING

Faithful men and women who love Jesus and who have faced alarming difficulties have had to face the ire, contempt and ridicule of men and women who claim to speak for God. Fredrick Pryce, Pastor of Word of Faith in Los Angeles is reputed as saying:

> ...how can you glorify God in your body, when it doesn't function right? How can you glorify God? How can He get glory when your body doesn't even work...? What makes you think the Holy Ghost wants to live inside a body where He can't see out through the windows and He can't hear with the ears? What makes you think the Holy Spirit

wants to live inside of a physical body where the limbs and the organs and the cells do not function right...? And what makes you think He wants to live in a temple where He can't see out of the eyes, and He can't walk with the feet, and He can't move with the hand...? The only eyes that he has that are in the earth realm are the eyes that are in the body. If He can't see out of them then God's gonna be limited he's not going to be helped....

Contrary to this doctrine that the Christian life is about tailor-made suits, designer clothes, limousines and airplanes, good physical and financial health, the Bible tends to offer a more balanced view.

Jesus admits, "I tell you the truth, no one who has left home or brothers or sisters or mother or father or children or fields for me and the gospel will fail to receive a hundred times as much in this present age (homes, brothers, sisters, mothers, children, and fields—and with them persecutions) and in the age to come eternal life" (Mark 11:29, 30).

Even in the context of being blessed a hundred fold as Jesus has promised, there is interlaced in this promise the un-doubted fact of persecution, tribulation, trials and hardship for the people of God who have given up everything to follow Him

Without understanding the importance of suffering, we may become fatalistic, resentful or resigned to our condition, and so our practice of the faith becomes legalistic, deterministic or duplicitous.

The elder brother in the story of the lost son is a classic case in point (Luke 15). He never complained to his father, he did his work dutifully. He never became immoral; no doubt his moral standards were very high. But he seethed with anger against his father. This came out at the return and the joyful accept-ance of the son once lost, but now found.

This second son, but elder brother, was locked in service without relationship. He saw his father as unfair and unkind, even though he would not directly admit it. He saw himself as righteous. He saw his brother as immoral and undeserving and he saw his service as a laborious and thankless drudgery.

This aspect of the parable shows how the Christian faith may be practiced with drudgery when the expectations are skewed and there is confusion in the practice of the faith.

No one, probably except the bizarre among us, likes to suffer and for most of us when we see suffering, it forces us to contemplate life's major issues. It concentrates our minds on such things as the purpose of life, the transience of our humanness and seeks to resolve issues of God's goodness and justice.

But Christians know what suffering is and none in the early church knew suffering as poignantly as Paul:

- We were under great pressure, far beyond our ability to endure, so that we despaired even for life (2 Cor. 1:8).
- ...As servants of God we commend ourselves in every way: in great endurance, in troubles, in hardships and distresses, in beatings, in imprisonments and riots; in hard work, sleepless nights and hunger; in purity, under- standing, patience and kindness; in the Holy Spirit and sincere love; in truthful speech and in the power of God; with weapons of righteousness in the right hand and in the left; through glory and dishonour, bad report and good report; genuine but regarded as impostors; known but regarded as unknown; dying and yet we live on; beaten and yet not killed; sorrowful, yet always rejoicing; poor, yet making many rich; having nothing, and yet pos- sessing everything (2 Corinthians 6:3-10).
- Five times I received from the Jews the forty lashes minus one. Three times I have been beaten with rods, once I was stoned, three times I was shipwrecked, I spent a night and a day in the open sea. I have been constantly on the move. I have been in danger from rivers, in danger from bandits, in danger from my own countrymen, in danger from Gen- tiles; in danger in the city, in danger in the country, in danger at sea, and in danger from false brothers. I have la-

boured and toiled and have often gone without sleep, I have known hunger and thirst and have often gone without food; I have been cold and naked. Besides everything else, I face daily the pressure of my concern for all the churches (2 Cor. 11:24-28).

Just reading Paul's autobiographical notes here in 2 Corinthians would make the most careful believer blush. As the writer in Hebrews 12:4 point out, "In your struggle against sin, you have not yet resisted to the point of shedding your blood."

And yet, Paul insists that among the things that he wanted to know was the fellowship of sharing in Jesus' sufferings and becoming like Him in His death (Philippians 3:10). Is Paul saying that despite all that he had faced there was more still to be faced? Is Paul throwing a perspective on the exercise and the demonstration of the faith that we miss or was this something not to be emulated but just unique to him?

Regrettably, this aspect of the call—suffering –to follow and to be like Jesus is sacrificed on the altar of a sanitised Christianity. It is a tragedy, that so much of Christianity demands good times, unlimited temporal blessings, healings, deliverances, and general freedom from challenges and problems. The songs of 'praise and worship' ("I'm next in line for my blessing," etc.) and much of the clichés of the faith (too blessed to be stressed, too anointed to be disappointment, etc.) are little more than grandiose spiritedness devoid of any understanding of the centrality of the cross of the faith.

Even our treatment of Philippians 4:13 ("I can do all things through Christ who gives me strength") is often times self-serving. The context is important:

I have learned to be *content* whatever the circumstances. I know what it is to be in need, and I know what it is to have plenty. I have learned the secret of being *content* in any and every situation, whether well fed or hungry, whether living in plenty or in want. I can do everything through him who gives me strength *(italics added)*.

This is the lesson on the strength of contentment that God gives in good times and in bad times, whether full or hungry, whether in plenty or in want. Paul was saying that God has granted him the power of contentment to face all my life circumstances, not an unrestricted power to act in one's own interest about being rich and popular and famous!

Do not misunderstand, for the faith does not call us to be 'sufferers' or make us 'sufferers.' It declares us sons, more than conquerors, victorious etc, but it is not to be understood as the world does, rather, it must be held in constant tension as epitomised in Paul's autobiographical note in 2 Corinthians 11:27. "I have laboured and toiled and have often gone without sleep, I have known hunger and thirst and have often gone without food; I have been cold and naked."

It does not seem that Paul chose these things for himself, but rather that in the cut and thrust of living out his faith, these became his experiences marking a necessary consequence of the practice of that faith demonstrating the power of contentment.

This biblical model demands and requires that those who are going to be followers of Jesus must know and clearly appropriate in their thinking the probability, indeed, the likelihood that their faith will be challenged with rigorous tests that God will permit for His sovereign glory.

The fact is serious believers will come under pressure in several of the ways that the apostle has described. He does not paint a life of ease and comfort for the believer, but one of hardships and trials. We must be careful then how we insist that God must fulfil His promises to us. The agenda must remain His and His alone. The believer will endeavour to understand that God is about bringing us to obedience in Christ that we might reflect His glory in everything.

THE SOURCE OF SUFFERING

The faith that Christians are called to is one which necessitates suffering. It is suffering because it is conflict. It is conflict against the sinful nature, and Paul describes that conflict so well in Romans 7. It is conflict against the world systems and structures and philosophies. Both John and James warn against the spiritual dangers that the world poses. This requires that the Christian be counter-cultural, subversive even, and this sometimes costs in immense ways. It is conflict against principalities and powers and here sometimes there may be serious suffering.

What is clear is that the principle of suffering for the Christian is to be understanding, not so much in the embracing of the disciplines—fasting, solitude, meditation etc., but in the fact of being and living in a world that is under the control of the evil one. He is called the god of this world and as such his systems and strategies are always to disrupt the work of God and to destroy the people of God. Christians are not of this world, they belong to another kingdom, with a different value system, with a different point of reference for life and meaning.

Jesus makes the point well. He says, "In this world you will have trouble..." (John 16:33). The trouble affects us at all levels, physically, emotionally and spiritually. Paul says, "Let no one cause me trouble, for I bear in my body the marks of Jesus" (Galatians 6:17). Whatever else he may have meant by this, it is clear that this apostle was physically scarred for his faith in Jesus.

The believer does not belong to this world; he is a square peg in a round hole. That is why Jesus taught her to pray for deliverance from evil and that is why He in turn prayed that they would be protected in the world (John 17:15).

Jesus' prayer for protection for the believers implies that they are in potential danger and that they cannot safeguard themselves by their efforts from this danger. This requires divine intervention.

JESUS HAD TO SUFFER

In our understanding of the faith, we must appreciate that suffering was a necessary part of the life of Jesus. He explains in Luke 24:25, 26 that He had to suffer. The prophets had declared it. And the same idea is conveyed in Acts 17:3.

The point is significant because the Jews did not expect that Messiah would suffer. In their own thinking, He was the Son of God and could be subject to nothing or to anyone. The idea of Him suffering was preposterous. And many believers have come to believe this too. The idea that they should suffer is held as preposterous because Jesus suffered for them, and as beneficiaries of His passion they will not have to face anything that He faced.

In the view of many, any suffering that may come their way cannot be of God, because it is God's will for them to prosper and to be in good health! Or by His stripes we are healed! How tragic that these texts have been used to humiliate God's people who know nothing of the "prosperity and the good health" that some so dangerously teach!

What the Scriptures reveal very clearly is that Jesus Christ, though being very God, had to suffer. And this suffering was fully intended to bring His Father glory. The same is true for the believer. He too will have to suffer and the suffering that he faces is intended to bring glory to God.

SUFFERING BRINGS DEPENDENCE UPON GOD

And so the same theme of suffering flows over in the lives of the believers. Paul describes it in 2 Corinthians 1:3–11 in which he explains that suffering is necessary that we might learn to depend upon God and not on ourselves (9).

In his own experience, he talks of suffering as being weakened so that he might find his strength in God. The point here is the fact that the crucified life brings us to total and unequivocal dependence upon God. None is made perfect in his walk of faith until suffering takes him to take complete and absolute hold of God. The troubles of the Christian life are designed to bring us to closer faith and trust in God who promises to live through us and thereby bring glory to Himself.

CHRISTLIKENESS INCLUDES SUFFERING

Paul continues the thought by arguing for the need to become like Christ by sharing in His suffering (Philippians 3:7–10). Christlikeness then includes sharing in the suffering of Christ. It includes facing aloneness in the crowd, it means dependence on God to meet all needs, and it means personal powerlessness as one is being drained of his own strength. It is a difficult proposition, but a necessary one for all who would live the crucified life.

In Hebrews 2:10, the author explains there that Jesus was made perfect through His suffering. This is not to suggest that Jesus had any imperfection in Himself. The point of the text is that Jesus' life mission could not have been completed without participating in and enduring suffering. God made Jesus perfect, in the sense of the completion of His mission, through suffering. His natural life began with suffering and it ended at the cross with suffering.

And throughout His life, he had to face suffering as well. We sometimes limit suffering only to having to face martyrdom and imprisonment. But Hebrews 2:18 explains that Jesus faced suffering when He was tempted. We normally see Jesus as breezing through His temptation episodes as though they had no effect upon Him. But while He knew no sin, it is clear that some of the temptation episodes that He faced were very bruising encounters so much so that angels had to minister to him after He withstood them.

Bear in mind that because of who He was the temptations that were set before Him were far deeper than anything that the believer could face. The believer has not had to face temptations to the degree that Jesus did.

·　·　·　·　·

INCARNATIONAL SUFFERING

On this point too, there is a vicarious effect to suffering. Jesus suffered to make men holy. If we begin to see the act of suffering as an opportunity to help to bring transformation to those under sin and oppression, then we will begin to see suffering in a whole new light.

Jesus suffered to bring that kind of response to humanity. Human beings tend to be sentimentally drawn to those who have been wounded by life and those who care for them. Our greatest admiration is reserved for those who have had to face great odds and challenges and in the face of them are still able to triumph and to see life not as drudgery, but as a joy, a chance to improve the lot of others.

The writer of Hebrews stresses this point in Hebrews 10:32-39. There he talks about believers who in the early days fought in the great contest in the face of great suffering. They not only suffered loss of property and exposure to insult and persecution, but they stood side by side with those who were suffering similar situations.

Here in the West, that type of persecution is generally yet unknown, but there is no doubt that it shall come. Churches will be losing their properties; individual believers will be forced to give up their property. Some will face hardship, persecution, imprisonment and loss just as fellow believers elsewhere have had to endure and are enduring. We must not suppose that because we are in the 'free' West, that such things will not happen to us. It shall come upon the Western church as night follows day and the believers must be prepared.

MODELLING SUFFERING

The first epistle of Peter spends quite a bit of time on the subject of suffering. In 1:6 the writer makes the point that the believers then had had to suffer many trials 'for a little while.'

In the text dealing with how slaves should respond to their masters, Peter makes an astounding comment. He argues there that it is commendable if a man bears up under the pain of unjust suffering because he is conscious of God (2:19). And nobody displayed this better than Jesus Christ on the cross. He endured the mockery of a trial, His Roman judge found Him innocent and yet, He was ordered crucified. The commendation in the case of Jesus was that in the face of His unjust suffering He was conscious of God and that consciousness, never left Him.

Consciousness of God in the face of suffering is the greatest asset that anyone can have and hold on to. Peter repeats the Pauline theme that the Christian is called to the crucified life. He explains in 1 Peter 2:20, 21 that the Christian has been called to suffer because Jesus suffered for him and left him an example that he should follow in His steps. Following in the steps of Jesus involves suffering. The way of Jesus is the way of suffering, not because it is sought after, but because assuming Christ necessarily assumes suffering. Assuming Christ is assuming the cross of Christ. Jesus says that following Him requires taking up the cross daily (Matthew 16:24; Luke 9:23).

Suffering as Purification

Peter also explains another important aspect of the magnitude of suffering. In 1 Peter 4:1 he says there that the person who has suffered in his body is done with sin. This is difficult to understand, but looking back at the cross, the death of Jesus meant that He was no longer subject to temptation, or to the wear and tear of the vagaries of this life. Paul explains this in Romans 6. The person who is crucified is by that death given the capacity to live the way God wants him to live. He is no longer a slave of sin and is no longer subject to its automatic and irresistible dictates. It is only when the believer is crucified that he begins to find true victory over sin. Where the believer finds himself susceptible to a particular sin, he has not yet crucified himself in that area.

According to Romans 6, Paul explains this in two senses: the believer is to offer his whole body to Christ, but he must also offer the parts of his body to Christ (6:13, 19). My spiritual mentor, Rev. Courtney Richards, has been very strong on this point. The one is as important as the other. In a whole or total sense, through faith we come to belong to Him, and yet, we must resist the anxiety to recoil into ourselves when we are forced to face the challenges of life.

We may therefore understand that what the apostle has here in mind is that suffering serves as a means of our inner purification. He argues that since Christ suffered in His body, He is done with sin—He dealt sin a death blow. We then, when we suffer are being brought to rely on God, and change our spirit perspective to live not according to the sin nature, but according to the Spirit of God in us.

Just as at the crucifixion, Jesus commended the keeping of His spirit to His Father, so according to Peter, when Christians suffer according to the will of the Father, they are to commit their keeping to a faithful God (1 Peter 4:19).

Even the benediction of his work emphasises suffering. In 5:10 he says—"And the God of all grace, who called you to his eternal glory in Christ, *after you have suffered a little while will himself restore you and make you strong, firm and steadfast. To him be the power forever and ever."* Amen. (*Italics added)* What a very sobering benediction!

SUFFERING AS PATERNAL DISCIPLINING

Of course, there is also suffering as disciplining, or as chastening. If we are God's children, He reserves the right to discipline us towards our spiritual restoration. God's heavy hand of punishment upon the believer is never only punitive, but always restorative. It is those who are rebellious and unrepentant in discipline who eventually are left alone in the quagmire of their ignorance. God never intends that any of His children should be left in that condition.

When God punished Miriam, she had to stay outside of the camp, and the whole camp had to wait until she was healed before they could move again. So even in the case of God's judgment upon the believer, it is always with a view to bring him to his senses that he might live the way God wants Him to so that the erring one may return to the community and move on in and with the community (Num. 12:14-16).

PAUL'S THORN IN THE FLESH (2 COR. 12:7-10)

Paul talks also of a thorn in his flesh, a messenger of Satan to keep him from taking pride or becoming prideful from what God allowed him to experience. This is a most telling text.

Paul explains that fourteen years ago, God allowed him into paradise or the third heaven and showed him some things there that no human lips can express. He says that God showed him such visions and revelations that would boggle the mind. Obviously, any believer would be excited by these things and probably would be disposed to feel particularly uniquely special at the privilege. It was indeed a unique privilege but to keep the apostle from making that experience the source of his faith in God, God allowed Satan to inflict some wound upon him.

He had been carrying this condition for over fourteen years! Here he was, fourteen years later, carrying the condition, reminding himself that God's grace was stronger than the torment which led to the weakness that he carried.

We can only speculate as to what this weakness might have been. In Gal.3:13 -16 it seems that Paul had serious problems with his sight, so serious that he was at risk of being treated with scorn.

Or is Romans 7 a none-too-veiled admission of Paul concerning his personal struggle with the sin nature? He says there, "What I do is not the good I want to do; no, the evil I do not want to do—this I keep on doing." He says, "In my inner being I delight in God's law, but I see another law at work in the members of my body, waging war with the law of my mind and making me a prisoner of the law of sin at work in my members."

Or was it that there was something about his appearance which made him come across as weak and uninviting? It seems that his detractors argued this way. They said that his letters were strong, but he was weak and frail in appearance (2 Cor. 10:1, 10).

In any event, what he faced was serious enough for him to ask God to take it away. But he also knew the reason that God allowed him that thorn. It was his to keep and it was intended to keep the apostle from boasting of something he experienced fourteen years previously. The point is this, what God will not save us from He will keep us through by His grace.

PILGRIMAGE AS SUFFERING

The scriptures seem to indicate that we suffer by being in a world that is simply hostile to us. We can't live and enjoy kingdom life and kingdom principles as we would like in a hostile environment. Under the strain of their own suffering, the people of Israel in exile asked themselves, 'how shall we sing the Lord's song in a strange land?' The Christian cannot ask that question. He must sing the Lord's song, even in a strange land. The land might not like to hear it, but it must be done.

Further, the writer in Hebrews says that the world does not deserve the people of God. It says, "...some faced jeers and flogging while others were chained and put in prison. They were stoned; they were sawed in two; they were put to death by the sword. They went about in sheepskins and goatskins, destitute, persecuted, and mistreated—the world was not worthy of them" (Heb. 13:36–38).

If more Christians were living as strangers and pilgrims in the land rather than as citizens at ease in the land, then the sharpness of the suffering that they would have to face would be more telling. Christian suffering on a whole is not as obvious because in many instances, Christianity has been compromised by believers who have not made the distinction in their lives of being in the world, and not of the world, of living by the Spirit and not by the flesh and knowing the wiles of the devil and not giving him a foothold. In Ezekiel God laments the rising 'endarkenment' in Israel, the profaning of God, acts committed by the priesthood—"Her priests do violence to my law and profane my holy things; they do not distinguish between the holy and the common; they teach that there is no difference between the unclean and the clean; and they shut their eyes to the keeping of my Sabbaths, so that I am profaned among them" (Ezekiel 22:26).

TEMPTATION AS SUFFERING

Jesus suffered when He was tempted, so we too suffer when we are tempted. The bombardments of the world, the flesh and the devil will take a toll upon us and as a result we hurt, we are alienated, we are treated as incompetent, others are promoted over us, moral and ethical traps are set for us and all kinds of divers schemes are set to keep us down and rob us of the equality of dignity with others.

LIVING COUNTER-CULTURALLY AS SUFFERING

Another means by which we suffer is by way of the extra precautions we must take in the face of the challenges that we face. That is why Paul makes the point that if Christianity were ever found to be untrue, we would be of all men most wretched. We live with an eternal perspective, not a temporal one. Our lives are lived not out of self-interest, but have the glory of God and the serving of others as the constant theme. This is inner difficulty. It goes against the natural flow of our instinct. We suffer as Christians and are thought to be less wise than the people of the world. For instance, we, by our very nature must clearly and indisputably keep the law of the land; we must not break it, even if those who make it disregard it. In the eyes of the world, we are shafted by our obedience, while those who break it advance at our expense.

We live with a different point of reference—It is never about us, nor our comfort, nor our security. It is always about Him and how His glory is manifest in us. Our salvation experience must first be understood against the background of God, His plan, His will, His purposes, rather than ourselves. While salvation is critical in God's revelation of Himself, it is not central. Salvation remains a part of the overall plan of God. Salvation is first about God's glory before it is about our blessing. It is God who must be the central theme—God the Personal Being!

The book of the Revelation echoes with that perpetual refrain:

- "You are worthy, our Lord and God, to receive glory and honor and power, for you created all things, and by your will they were created and have their being" (Rev. 4:11).
- In a loud voice they sang: "Worthy is the Lamb, who was slain, to receive power and wealth and wisdom and strength and honour and glory and praise!" (Rev. 5:12)
- All the angels were standing around the throne and around the elders and the four living creatures. They fell down on their faces before the throne and worshiped God, saying: "Amen! Praise and glory and wisdom and thanks and honour and power and strength be to our God for ever and ever. Amen!" (Rev. 7:11,12)

The point is this, heaven is not about us, but rather it is about Him. Our practice of the faith in this life is to be lived in light of that reality, where our energies are spent God-centred rather than self-centred.

LEARNING HARD LESSONS

Suffering occurs when God wants us to learn something that we have difficulty learning. Sometimes the process of learning may be tedious, and we get hard knocks along the way. He is not intending to destroy us in the process. His intention is that we might be restored and that we might function at a higher purposive level.

Hagar had to learn this lesson. She runs away in the face of her suffering and hardship. God meets her in the desert. Listen to the conversation in Genesis 16:7-9.

And he said, "Hagar, servant of Sarai, where have you come from, and where are you going?" "I'm running away from my mistress Sarai," she answered. Then the angel of the LORD told her, "Go back to your mistress and submit to her."

No doubt, this was extremely difficult for Hagar to have heard. She was to return to the woman who was mistreating her. She was pregnant and she felt tired, lonely and abused. Of course she seemed to have forgotten her role in the ordeal as well. She had been bragging on Sarai because she was bearing Abraham's child and made no bones about it.

In her privileged position she became arrogant and self centred. She would mercilessly provoke Sarai with the fact that *she* was carrying the child and not Sarai.

Sarai began to react to the constant goading until it became a serious crisis in the family. Accusations and counter-accusations, recriminating and blaming became the order of family life.

Abraham placed the blame for everything on Sarai, who took matters in her own hands to shield herself from further pain, shame and hurt. Sarai began to treat the pregnant Hagar quite badly. After all, she was still a slave, her slave!

And Hagar ran. God tells her to go back to sort out the foundational issue of life—relationships! How do we respond when we face the tensions in relationships as there was between Hagar and Sarai, Sarai and Abraham, Abraham and Hagar?

What do we do when our joy in a relationship turns to pain? What do we do when the pleasure we experienced suddenly turns to ashes in our mouths? What do we do when the security that we thought we had is suddenly pulled from under us and we are left vulnerable, exposed? Sometimes God sends us back to the place of pain so that we might understand the importance of the power of crucifixion. What God will not save us from He will safely take us through as long as we stay crucified.

THE DIVINE BOAST AND SUFFERING

There is also the divine boast. Job encountered this, and believers throughout the centuries have undergone this type of trial. The scriptures explain that the believer is God's workmanship which God puts on display to the universe from time to time (Eph. 2:9ff). In the display of His workmanship, the accuser will come before God to seek to separate God from His workmanship. This was the attempt that he made against Job. He told God that Job was only serving Him for what he could get. God was confident that such was not the case and so Job was put through amazing pain and suffering. Probably, outside of the life of Jesus the person in the scriptures who seemed to have physically suffered most is Job, to say nothing of his emotional and spiritual pain.

Look at some of the things that happened to him:

- Job was so disfigured by the malady that he was barely recognisable (Job 2:7, 19:19).
- He had sores all over his body. He used a piece of pottery to scrape himself as he sat in the ashes (Job 2:7,8).
- When he laid down at nights, it was torturous as he twisted and turned sleeplessly wishing for day to break (7:4).
- Apparently his wounds were infected by and infested with worms (7:5).
- He lost weight and became skin and bones (19:20).
- His breath became offensive (19:17).
- His skin became black and would peel off (30:30).
- He had fever (30:30).
- Boys unhesitatingly spat in his face (30:10).
- He was in constant pain (30:17).

God boasted concerning Job. He was confident of the integrity of Job's life. Satan tried to separate God from Job by accusing Job quite falsely before God. To prove to Satan that Job was not as he said, God placed Job in Satan's hands to do with him as pleased him with the proviso not to touch Job's life.

And what a contest it proved to be—the emotional pain that Job went through was immense, the mocking, the insults, the shame, the loss of position, the loss of possession; all these must have been dreadful.

The spiritual pain was undoubtedly great—his sense of confusion at God, the accusation of his friends that he must have sinned and was being punished by God, the godless suggestion of his wife to curse God and die, all of these boiled up in an awful cup of bitterness to drink confirming his faithfulness to God.

PHYSICAL SUFFERING

Suffering may also be physical, when in the process of obeying God we are physically affected. Believers in some places find themselves in prison, or under house arrest. Some are killed for their faith. These physical attacks are not as prevalent in our part of the vineyard. What have been generally observed on the physical side of things are effects of demonic activities against believers. Some have had their property stolen; some have been in life-threatening accidents; some have been harassed at airports etc.

There are some insights to learn from the life of Moses in the synopsis given in Hebrews 11:24-29. The greater the call of faith in the crucified life the greater the suffering and trial one has to face.

Evidently, Moses always knew who he was even though he was in Pharaoh's house. So when he came of age, he renounced his adopted Egyptian heritage preferring rather to be known as an Israelite. Note that the author says there that Moses preferred disgrace for the sake of Christ rather than to enjoy Egypt's fine pleasures.

What would Moses have known about Christ? There is an inner reality for the people of God which are known and discovered not in the response to the natural, but in the affirmation of the spiritual.

Further, there are times when believers have unexplainable illnesses. Doctors can't say what the causes there may be. Sometimes it may well be that the devil is trying to separate God from the believer through the inflicting of physical pain.

SUFFERING AS DEPENDENCE (2 COR 1:3-11)

In probably the most autobiographical of all of Paul's letters, we get to see glimpses of how He lived as a Christian. Already quoted above are some of the things that he endured. In the text above, Paul is making the point that suffering is intended to build in us a sense of reliance upon God. Christianity demands reliance upon God or faith in Him and one of the ways that God ensures that faith in Him is fortified is by way of the cross.

In this text, Paul praises God, describing Him as the God of all comfort and the Father of compassion. He says that God comforts us in troubles so that when we are in trouble we can be of comfort to others. The text may be addressing the pain that comes in being faithful to Jesus, in walking with Him and in honouring Him. It is a reminder to believers that the agony of such experiences is to serve as grounding for others who may go through similar trials.

But it may also serve as a lesson to brothers and sisters who have fallen in various ways and who through God's comfort find restoration and so can comfort others. The faith also encounters falling and failing, the need for forgiveness and the hand of reconciliation and so, those thus restored may assure others that there is hope.

He continues by pointing out that as much as suffering overflows to others, comfort also overflows. Both comforting the wounded and modelling suffering flow from Jesus and they flow to those who find themselves in that situation so that those in suffering could also experience comfort from those around who had gone through similar suffering.

Paul points out further that the distress he was undergoing was not so much for his benefit as it was for the salvation of the Corinthians. The comfort that he encountered too, was not his either, but rather, that they might model endurance during suffering, just as those before them did.

Paul then addresses the personal sufferings that he had to endure and points out to the Corinthians that it was so intense that he thought he would have died. He explains here that the intensity of this suffering taught him not to depend upon any-thing or anyone else but upon God. After all, the same God who allowed suffering is the same God who could provide the miracle of His comfort in the face of suffering. What this points to and reminds us of is that the believer's point of refer-ence in all things is to be Christ.

In the midst of trial, there is only One who has delivered and will deliver. Paul understood this. The reminder in trial is that God is both the source of comfort in trial and deliverance from trial. He keeps us in trial and He saves us from trial. Any attempt to find comfort elsewhere or deliverance elsewhere circumvents the very plan of God in regards to this important purpose of suffering, for it is intended to show God as both comforter and deliverer.

As I have tried to show, Christians suffer in many ways. Paul argues from this text that suffering is to accomplish several things, but highlights the fact that the suffering of Christ flows over into the life of the believer. The person then who is not yet encountering the suffering of Christ might not yet begin to live the Christian life. It is a necessary and an inescapable part of it.

But Paul also wants to highlight that in the midst of suffering, God provides others around to offer help and encouragement either by way of their positive and affirming and comforting action or else by way of their prayers.

But the fundamental point that the apostle seeks to establish here is that regardless of how deep the suffering is, it must be understood that that suffering must bring us away from self reliance to reliance upon the Holy Spirit through faith.

SUFFERING AND THE GLORY OF GOD

In John 11, there is described the story of the sickness and the death of Lazarus. After learning of the sickness of Lazarus, Jesus calmly comments that this sickness and the eventual death of Lazarus—"This sickness will not end in death. No, it is for God's glory so that God's Son may be glorified through it."

God was to be glorified through the sickness and death of Lazarus. Is this only to be understood in the immediate sense of the text, that Lazarus was to be brought back from the dead, or is there still the demonstration of the glory of God in the sickness and death of those whom Jesus loves?

It is a most difficult proposition especially for those who must watch their loved ones suffer. What in suffering is there to bring glory to God? How does the loss of a limb, the breaking down of the body by some malignant disease, the non-functioning of some vital organ of the body bring glory to Him, especially when in the Old Testament economy that which was damaged, broken, or somehow paralysed could not be presented?

The LORD said to Moses the following:

Say to Aaron: "For the generations to come none of your descendants who has a defect may come near to offer the food of his God. No man who has any defect may come near: no man who is blind or lame, disfigured or deformed; no man with a crippled foot or hand, or who is hunchbacked or dwarfed, or who has any eye defect, or who has festering or running sores or damaged testicles. No descendant of Aaron the priest who has any defect is to come near to present the offerings made to the LORD by fire. He has a defect; he must not come near to offer the food of his God. He may eat the most holy food of his

God, as well as the holy food; yet because of his defect, he must not go near the curtain or approach the altar, and so desecrate my sanctuary. I am the LORD, who makes them holy" (Lev. 21-16-23).

And yet Jesus saw His own suffering and death in John 12 as bringing glory to God. He says in chapter 12:23-28.

The hour has come for the Son of Man to be glorified. I tell you the truth, unless a kernel of wheat falls to the ground and dies, it remains only a single seed. But if it dies, it produces many seeds. The man who loves his life will lose it, while the man who hates his life in this world will keep it for eternal life. Whoever serves me must follow me; and where I am, my servant also will be. My Father will honor the one who serves me. "Now my heart is troubled, and what shall I say? 'Father, save me from this hour? No, it was for this very reason I came to this hour. Father, glorify your name!' Then a voice came from heaven, 'I have glorified it, and will glorify it again.'"

The same issue is raised regarding the man born blind in John 9. The disciples assumed that the man's blindness was because of either his own sin (strange, since evidently he was born that way) or because of his parents' sins (a generational consequence of sins). Jesus assured them that neither was the case. He was that way, so that God's work may be displayed in Him.

Would the work of God still be displayed in this man if Jesus did not heal him? Would it have been the consequences of his own sins, or the sins of his parents if Jesus did not restore his sight? It seems that this man's life was intended by God to bring Him glory however God decided.

Again, there is no question that God being glorified in our pain is a difficult proposition. It raises more questions than we cannot satisfactorily answer. Perhaps the best answer is to be found in Paul's powerful dictum on life's circumstances found in Romans 8.

And we know that in all things God works for the good of those who love him, who have been called according to his purpose. For those God foreknew he also predestined to be conformed to the likeness of his Son, that he might be the firstborn among many brothers. And those he predestined, he also called; those he called, he also justified; those he justified, he also glorified (Rom. 8:26-30).

Perhaps the text is hinting at our conforming to the image of Jesus through the working together of all things in our lives including suffering. Think of the great Christian artiste Joni Eareckson-Tada, who as a result of a diving accident, was left a quadriplegic in a wheelchair who in her work *The God I Love* says "...we will stand amazed to see the topside of the tapestry and how God beautifully embroidered each circumstance into a pattern for our good and His glory." In the same work she says, "Sometimes God allows what he hates to accomplish what he loves."

Or think even with equal amazement of Nick Vujicic, the Australian, born without hands or legs and who has been making great strides for the kingdom of God. Nick Vujicic has made the astonishing point that "If God can use a man without arms and legs to be His hands and feet, then He will certainly use any willing heart!"

Perhaps one last observation is important here. The world is full of suffering. Human suffering is well documented and well known. If suffering by itself were to make the world a better place, then indeed, the world would have been a better place. For those of us as believers, we must see suffering in the wider context of the hand of God, not as something that He cherishes, but as something which the surrendered life will give back to Him to use for His purposes. It is the way of the cross. The cross takes the suffering of the world and makes it into a bouquet of God's grace, to the praise of His glory. It is that willingness to give God the brokenness of our lives which gives suffering new meaning.

4.

THE POSITIONAL BLESSINGS OF JESUS' CRUCIFIXION

But we see Jesus, who was made a little lower than the angels, now crowned with glory and honour, because he suffered death, so that by the grace of God He might taste death for everyone (Heb. 2:9)

While the scriptures reveal a great number of truths about the benefits and the joys wrought to the believer by the death of Jesus no other book tells of its benefits in a more comprehensive way than does the book of Hebrews. So I will depend largely on this book to identify just some of the blessings that the crucifixion of Jesus brings to those who trust Him.

PURIFICATION FOR SINS (HEBREWS 1:3)

In the Old Testament, purification remained a strong motif. Under the Levitical rules, the priest had to be purified before he could perform the duties of his office. He could not come to perform His duties except that he were purified. He had to be purified both by water and by blood.

In Leviticus 8 at the ordination of Aaron and his sons as priests, they had to be washed with water and then had oil poured over them, then they had blood applied to the lobes of their ears, the thumbs of their right hands and the big toes of their right feet.

This symbol as set out in Leviticus 8 points to the preparation of the believer through the purification of Christ for service at the altar unto Him.

TASTING OF DEATH FOR EVERYONE (HEBREWS 2:9)

Among the strongest theological themes of the scriptures is the message that the wages of sin is death. From Adam in Genesis 2 to those described as dogs in Revelation 22, the sentence is the same. Death and separation from God are the natural lot of all men. Life then is impossible for men who constantly live in sin and who carry its sentence upon their shoulders.

HIS DEATH DESTROYED THE DEVIL (HEBREWS 2:15)

The song writer who penned "up from the grave He arose, with a mighty triumph o'er His foes" did not get it quite right. Jesus triumphed over the devil, not at the resurrection, but at the cross. When He cried, "it is finished!" He meant it. Satan was defeated at the cross not in the tomb.

Further, this text points out that Jesus shared in our humanity , so that by His death He might destroy him who holds the power of death—that is, the devil—and free those who all their lives were held in slavery by their fear of death. So for the believer, death carries no special fear. It has lost both its sting and its victory. Indeed, believers who die are described as asleep, since the fear of death is broken.

The fear of death is replaced by the perfect love of Christ in the believer for through Christ's perfect love in us, that which stung Him once, has no ability to hurt anyone, anymore.

ATONEMENT (HEBREWS 2:17)

At the cross, Jesus secured our peace. God's will is that the enmity that exists between the earth and the throne-room would cease. In the death of Jesus He tore down the middle wall of partition which separated people from each other and which separated God from the people.

His death brought unparalleled peace. Those who were afar off have been brought near and those who were at enmity have changed their weapons of war into tools for living.

ETERNAL REDEMPTION (HEBREWS 9:12)

In the cross of Jesus Christ is to be found eternal redemption. This points to the great price incurred by human captivity to sinful nature, to the world and to the devil being fully paid for. Only the blood of Jesus could bring this about.

David commands his soul to praise the Lord who redeems his soul from destruction and crowns it with love and compassion (Psalm 103:4). Redemption is both from something and to something. Redemption is from death to life, from war to peace, from darkness to light and from transgression to holiness.

Not only that, but the quality of the redemption is to be noted. It is described here as eternal redemption, which means that its effect is beyond time. It is everlasting. It is a final and irrevocable purchase.

CLEANSED CONSCIENCES (HEBREWS 9:14)

This text clearly teaches that at the cross Jesus empowers the believer to live in faith, not from a conscience which only acts with reason and cultural trappings. Consciences are cleansed from acts that lead to death by the blood of Jesus.

The Bible describes several possible characteristics of the conscience:

- A pure conscience (1 Tim. 3:9, 2 Tim. 1:3)
- The good conscience (Acts 23:1,1 Tim. 1:5,19; Heb. 13:8, 1 Pet. 3:16, 21)
- The conscience void of offence or a clear conscience (Acts 24:16, 1 Cor. 4:4)
- The conscience which bears witness or a confirming

conscience (Rom. 2:15, 9:1, 2 Cor. 1:12)
- The weak and defiled conscience (1 Cor. 8:7–10)
- A seared conscience (1 Tim. 4:2)
- An evil conscience (Heb. 10:22)

The conscience, though innate, is largely a creature of conditioning. Depending on the factors that may be brought to bear on it, the conscience may lack the kind of decisiveness it needs to help the individual make morally sound decisions. This is not in regards to salvation, but in regards to how persons may relate to each other and how a person may relate to himself. By itself it cannot make spiritual judgments.

In 1 Cor. 4:4 Paul makes the important point that a clear conscience does not make a person innocent before God, because the purpose of conscience is to give moral, not spiritual direction.

The most significant thing about the gift of a cleansed conscience is that it saves someone from thinking that moral uprightness might bring salvation and points that person to serving God. The conscience which has not been cleansed in this way, will at best seek to find moral ways to please God without truly surrendering to God.

THE SACRIFICE OF HIMSELF DOES AWAY WITH SIN (HEBREWS 9:26)

When Jesus went to the cross and He sacrificed Himself, He settled every question of sin, so that those who live in Him would be empowered to live beyond acts of the sin nature, beyond the deception of the world and beyond the allure of false spirits.

In His death, there is no need for a repeat performance. It was an all-sufficient, efficacious and decisive act. In this death, no further sacrifice is necessary. Every animal, sheep, goat, bull, pigeon or dove may now breathe a sigh of relief, for no subsequent sacrifice for sin is required.

The issue of sin is settled in the death of Jesus Christ upon the cross and it serves as the point of reference for everyone wounded by sin. The cross is the final and decisive answer to the issue of sin.

CRUCIFIXION TAKES AWAY THE SINS OF MANY PEOPLE (HEBREWS 9:28)

The scriptures teach that sin's wages is death. It also teaches that left by ourselves, we would never be either willing to or able to pay for it. It is in Christ Jesus that the matter is settled. He did this by shedding His blood upon Calvary's tree.

HOLINESS BY THE ONCE FOR ALL SACRIFICE OF JESUS (HEBREWS 10:10, 29; 13:12)

Not only has the question of atonement been settled, but by crucifixion, Jesus procured holiness for those who would be saved. In the cross He took upon Himself sin and at the cross, He bequeathed to all who would trust Him, the holiness of God. The fact is as Paul puts it, He who did not know sin, became sin for us, so that in Him, we might become the right-eousness of God.

Theologians wrangle, as they usually do over many things, about what it means that He became sin. Was He the sin-bearer of Leviticus or did He actually become the embodiment of sin? Whatever the conclusions drawn, the fact is that in Jesus' sacrificing Himself He knew that it was a sacrifice that would once for all make those who appropriated it, holy.

PERFECTION FOREVER FOR THOSE BEING MADE HOLY (HEBREWS 10:15)

The point is pushed even further by this text, for it teaches that perfection for the believer comes by way of the crucifixion of Jesus Christ. This stretches even further what the previous verse discusses. Perfection is by way of the cross.

What the obvious emphasis by the writer of the Hebrews is here is that the cross satisfies every need that we could possibly have as human beings. It is an all-sufficient, satisfying and awesome act. Those who have come to the cross have already been made holy and have been perfected in Christ.

CONFIDENCE TO ENTER THE MOST HOLY PLACE (HEBREWS 10:19, 20)

This probably is the crescendo to the theme in the book of Hebrews of the effect of the crucifixion of Jesus Christ. Access to heaven is by the very cross of Jesus, for at the cross, He opened Himself that the redeemed might pass safely through Him to find fulfilment in God.

Heaven is the ultimate place of worship and it is entered by way of the body of Jesus and this is the way by which worship is made possible. This is the thought that the writer wants to build his final argument upon. In the Old Covenant worship was barely possible and certainly not open to all, not even all the redeemed, since only the priest could draw near in the sense of worship.

But here, all could draw near, not now to a temple made with human hands, but draw near by way of the broken body of Jesus. The celebration of the Lord's Supper is the most significant reminder of this great truth.

When the bread is broken and the cup is taken, the believer knows that he touches no ordinary thing. He understands by these symbols that he has been invited to the very Throne Room itself.

MODELLED IN CHRIST

What is true of Christ in His suffering must be true for the believer. The person who understands the crucified life also understands that that life is intended to bring hope, vitality and transformation to others. In the death of the self, it is others who reap the benefit of that death. When the believer by putting to death the misdeeds of the body begins to live a life of purity and true holiness, others around will benefit.

And when a believer, through the surrender of vulnerable personality traits, yield to the power of God then the impact of the kingdom becomes even more intense. This is because he is living with a certain degree of strengthened impregnability to the glory of God.

5.

CRUCIFIXION AND THE NEW CREATION

Therefore, if anyone is in Christ, he is a new creation; the old has gone, the new has come! (2 Cor.5:17)

It is the crucifixion of Jesus which has made the world of difference, quite literally, for those of us who have come to faith in Him. Make no mistake, the crucifixion of Jesus has served to redefine not only the natural realm, but the spiritual realm in fundamental and significant ways.

In a sense there has been a shift in God's dealing with mankind as a consequence of the crucifixion of Jesus Christ. It is the coming into being of a new world order. That new world order shifts the focus from man trying to please God through obedience under the Law, to God effecting salvation through faith in Jesus Christ alone, whose obedience is now imputed to all who believe. Paul puts it well in Gal. 2:19—For through the law I died to the law so that I might live for God.

Formerly men lived 'under the Law.' but now men live 'in Christ.' This is the new environment for all who are crucified. This is the realm of the spirit formerly kept hidden until faith should be revealed.

This is not to say that faith was not significant under the Old System of things, but men lived as spiritual prisoners until faith was revealed in Christ and by His crucifixion Jesus ushered in a new world.

It is a reality that the ancients longed to see, but never got to see. They were kept from receiving what was promised until the freedom of the new order should be effected through the cross of Jesus Christ.

There has been much debate about the relationship between the Old Covenant and the New. The purpose here is not to continue that debate, but rather to help us to see that as believers in the crucified Lord, we have been brought into newness of life in several significant ways.

The scriptures teach very clearly that the believer is "in Christ:"

- To the church of God in Corinth, to those sanctified in Christ Jesus and called to be holy, together with all those everywhere who call on the name of our Lord Jesus Christ—their Lord and ours (1 Cor. 1:20)
- There is neither Jew nor Greek, slave nor free, male nor female, for you are all one in Christ Jesus. (Gal. 3:28)
- And you also were included in Christ when you heard the word of truth, the gospel of your salvation. Having believed, you were marked in him with a seal, the promised Holy Spirit, (Eph. 1:13)

This moves the believer to function from a new point of reference in every way. God's New World has been manifest in the arrival of Christ and the establishment of His Kingdom.

A New Creation (2 Cor. 5:17)

In this regard then, the crucifixion has ushered in a new creation, a creation, not ordered on the natural things, but a creation ordered on spiritual things. The new creation sets out for the believer a new sphere of living, where the defining mode of living is by faith, not by sight.

The New Covenant teaches four defining things on faith:

- And without faith it is impossible to please God (Heb. 11:6).
- Everything that does not come from faith is sin (Rom. 14:23).

- We live by faith and not by sight (2 Cor. 5:7, Gal. 2:20).
- The only thing that counts is faith expressing itself through love (Gal. 5:6).

This faith is 'Faith in Christ' and this new place of being is 'in Christ.' This place of being, is described in several ways generally unknown to the saints of the Old Covenant.

The fact of the believer being 'in Christ' means that he lives life and views things not from the point of view of the world, but from the point of view of the Spirit. Paul says it this way:

And he died for all, that those who live should no longer live for themselves but for him who died for them and was raised again. So from now on we regard no one from a worldly point of view. Though we once regarded Christ in this way, we do so no longer. Therefore, if anyone is in Christ, he is a new creation; the old has gone, the new has come... We are therefore Christ's ambassadors... God made him who had no sin to be sin for us, so that in him we might become the righteousness of God (2 Cor. 5:14–21).

The text sets out three important points for us. In the first place, the death of Christ causes the believer to view life not from the realm of the world, but rather from the realm of the spirit.

Secondly, those who are in Christ are new creatures. The old is past, meaning, or at least suggesting, living from the point of view of the world has been shifted to living from the point of view of being in Christ.

The third observation is that those who are now in Christ live in the world not now as belonging to the world, but rather as ambassadors from Christ to the world with a ministry of reconciliation.

Those who are in Christ, live for Christ, from a position of being new creatures in Christ, sent back to the world not belonging to the world, but rather as ambassadors of Christ. The nature of an ambassador lies in that simple fact—he does not belong to the country in which he serves!

Again, Paul pulls faith, the new creation and crucifixion together in perfect beauty—For through the law I died to the law so that I might live for God. I have been crucified with Christ and I no longer live, but Christ lives in me. The life I live in the body, I live by faith in the Son of God, who loved me and gave himself for me (Gal. 2:19, 20)

A NEW ADAM (1 COR. 15:45)

All this is made possible because of the new Adam, Jesus Christ, whom the Bible calls the 'last Adam' (1 Cor. 15:45). The first Adam who belonged to the Old Order failed in so many ways. And where the two 'Adams' are concerned Paul explains the contrast between the two worlds with impeccable precision:

So it is written:'The first man Adam became a living being' the last Adam, a life-giving spirit. The spiritual did not come first, but the natural, and after that the spiritual. The first man was of the dust of the earth, the second man from heaven. As was the earthly man, so are those who are of the earth; and as is the man from heaven, so also are those who are of heaven. And just as we have borne the likeness of the earthly man, so shall we bear the likeness of the man from heaven (1 Cor. 15:45–49).

It is remarkable. In this regard therefore, the believer is freed from the first Adam and now lives in the image of the Last Adam. His life is empowered through the Life-giving-Adam rather than through the Life-receiving Adam. He is dead to that realm.

Through the first Adam his experience is sin and destruction, but through the last Adam, and now that He is living in the last Adam, since he is in Christ, he lives the life of the Spirit, since Christ lives in Him. A man cannot experience the life of the Spirit until he counts himself dead to that which flowed out of the first Adam.

A NEW LIGHT (2 COR. 4:6)

Not only that, the fact that the believer no longer lives under the rule of the First Adam nor under the rule of the Old Creation, he no longer function under the Old light. He is not defined by that which is natural, but by that which is eternal. The point of reference for life is not the light of the Sun, but indeed by the light of the Son.

As believers, the light we live by is not the light of the natural Sun, that is for natural men. We live by another light, from another world. Paul writes in 2 Cor. 4:6—For God, who said, "Let light shine out of darkness," made his light shine in our hearts to give us the light of the knowledge of the glory of God in the face of Christ!

What we carry in our hearts then is the light of the knowledge of the glory of God in the face of Christ. This whole world remains in darkness. It cannot see the light. "Let there be light!" takes on new significance for those who come into the new order of things into the new creation through the last Adam. The people of the world ruled by the First Adam, driven by that which is seen in the Old Order remained blind to real light, even though they have the light of the Sun.

But the scriptures teach us clearly that the god of this world has blinded them so that they cannot see that light (2 Cor. 4:4). God's creative shout in Genesis (1:3) becomes a redemptive shout here in 2 Corinthians. It heralds the fact that Jesus' crucifixion has made light possible in an unprecedented way.

See how closely the writer of the Hebrews equates receiving the light with suffering:

Remember those earlier days after you had received the light, when you stood your ground in a great contest in the face of suffering. Sometimes you were publicly exposed to insult and persecution; at other times you stood side by side with those who were so treated. You sympathized with those in prison and joyfully accepted the confiscation of your property, because you knew that you yourselves had better and lasting possessions (Heb. 10:32-34).

The crucifixion ushers in for us a new creation (the realm of the Spirit), a new light (the light of the knowledge of Jesus) through the last Adam (the life giving Spirit).

A NEW DAY (HEB. 3:7-8)

Here probably some may find their greatest challenge. Again this is not to raise an issue of a day of worship, but rather an attitude to service and worship. The new creation sets in motion a new day called 'Today' (Heb. 3:7, 8) which helps the people of God to understand that the light of the new creation does not go out. Revelation teaches us this very well. Under this light there is always opportunity for worship and there is always opportunity for service. There is always opportunity to spread the light of the knowledge of God.

"Today" redefines the calendar for the people of God for God is constantly at work in bringing the universe back to Himself. With the energy of the Spirit that He gives us, we are engaged in our spiritual today to fulfil all that God intends for us. And so the writer to the Hebrews says, "Today, if you hear his voice, do not harden your hearts..." This is the time for working, for fulfilling that which God intends in our lives.

In that sense today is to be understood as the space in which to fulfil our purpose, the reason why we have become the planting of the Lord, because tomorrow is promised to no one.

.   .   .   .   .

NEW WORSHIP (HEB. 11:22–24)

But you have come to Mount Zion, to the heavenly Jerusalem, the city of the living God. You have come to thousands upon thousands of angels in joyful assembly, to the church of the firstborn, whose names are written in heaven. You have come to God, the judge of all men, to the spirits of righteous men made perfect, to Jesus the mediator of a new covenant, and to the sprinkled blood that speaks a better word than the blood of Abel.

The writer of Hebrews contrasts the two worship experiences, the one under the Old Covenant and the other under the New. The contrasts are most instructive. The one tells of darkness, gloom and crippling fear, the other speaks of assurance, confidence and unspeakable joy.

Those who have come to be in Christ and who now live in Christ live in this way of joy for where the spirit of the Lord is there is liberty, a liberty practically unknown to the saints of the Old Covenant.

A NEW LAW (GAL. 3:25)

The new creation ushered in a new arrangement in a defining way. It takes man from under the Law and places him in Christ and under the law of Christ. Paul therefore says—To those under the law I became like one under the law (though I myself am not under the law), so as to win those under the law... (2 Cor. 9:20). Paul warned those with great sternness who wanted to be under the Law (Gal. 4:21) and described those who have returned to the Law and are seeking to be justified by the Law as having been alienated from Christ and fallen from grace (Gal. 5:4)!

It is a fundamental shift in the order of things. In the old way of thinking and living Paul explains in Galatians that the old creation was underpinned by slavery. Everyone was in slavery.

The Law remained the slave master, or the school teacher. He explains that now that Jesus died on the cross the promise of the Spirit has now been realised in a full way, faith in Christ satisfies the full demands of the Law which up to then left the whole world under a curse and now the way of to life is through faith in Christ which brings freedom in the spirit nullifying slavery under the Law.

Because of crucifixion, then, the believer has an unprecedented opportunity to live in the Spirit rather than under the Law. He has shifted his modus operandi from that which marks the Law of God to embracing the Spirit of God. It is not that the Law was useless; it was rather that it could not impart freedom or righteousness. Freedom and righteousness come by faith alone in Christ alone through the Spirit alone. The believer then now operates through the Spirit and in the Spirit rather than through the Law or by the Law.

The believer no longer functions under the dictates of the Old Order; he is born of the Second Adam and lives in the new light. This light is not the light of the natural order, but the light and the truth of the new order.

Old things are passed away means that he no longer lives according to the ways and systems of the former things, but he now lives in the realm of the spirit. He has been baptised with Christ and has been raised up to walk in the newness of life (Rom. 6:4).

A LIFE HIDDEN WITH CHRIST IN GOD (COL. 3:3)

The true life of the believer is hidden with Christ in God. This means that there is no possibility of being lost. A life hidden with Christ in God is a doubly indemnified life. Other scriptures support this. Jesus for instance talks about knowing His sheep and that no one can pluck them out of His hand or out of His Father's hand (John 10:27, 28). This 'no one' must necessarily include the sheep himself.

So the believer knows and understands that his security is guaranteed not because of what he does, but because of whose he is. He is a joint heir with Jesus with all the rights and privileges of that status (Rom. 8:17).

THE EVIL ONE CANNOT TOUCH HIM (1 JOHN 5:18)

Again, here is a most awesome declaration concerning the believer. His life is secure from the control and influence of all demonic principalities and powers. The demonic world understands who owns the believer and therefore knows that the believer is not his to even touch, much more to be held on to.

Jesus taught His disciples to pray for deliverance from the evil one (Luke 11:4) He Himself prayed that the believers might not be taken out of the world, but that they would be protected from the activities of the evil one (John 17:15).

MORE THAN A CONQUEROR (ROM. 8:37)

The believer walks not only in victory effected on his behalf, but himself is more than a conqueror. He actively participates in the triumph of all that opposes God and he subdues everything under his feet as Christ does.

Nothing can successfully revolt against him. He is absolutely and unequivocally in charge. Indeed, the believer shall reign with Christ and is reigning with Him, even as we speak. When Jesus who is our life shall appear, we too shall appear with Him in glory (Col. 3:4). That is the clear teaching of the scriptures, because already, as it is, the believer now shares Jesus' glory, the same glory (John 17:22) that God says that He would not share with anyone (Is. 48:11).

JUSTIFICATION

Every one of these views is absolutely true of the Christian. And it is important that they know them to be true. They add vim and vigour and a certain confidence in walking with the Lord.

John wrote to the saints that that may know that they have eternal life and that they might be confident in approaching God (1 John 5:13, 14). For these reasons then, it is important that the believer know his true position in the Lord.

What the believer has is summed up in the doctrine of justification. The doctrine of justification may be understood in the following analogy: It is like a man having been tried for the capital offence is found guilty by the judge. He is sentenced to death and is found sitting on death row. Another comes along, pleads to the judge on his behalf. He tells the judge that he would be willing to take the place of the convict on death row. The judge permits the appeal. This man goes to take the place of the man on death row. He is killed in the place of the guilty convict. The convicted man walks out of death row, not only free, but now bearing all the credentials, privileges and benefits of the man who dies in his place.

There is no record of the crime against him anymore, he cannot be charged with that crime, nor any other—he now has diplomatic immunity—he is not now subject to those things that once held him captive or which caused him to fall into sin and judgement. He will never face condemnation, ever!

This is the heart of the teaching of justification. It is that judicial and legally binding act of God in which He in the exercise of His prerogative as Judge declares everyone who places faith in Jesus Christ as absolutely and irrevocably free. He is not only made free, but his status has been changed. Every record of his former self is erased and he becomes a new creature. He is no longer under the jurisprudence of the Old System, but now lives in the very place of the privileges of Jesus.

There are several texts which identify the believer as already justified before God:

- Through him, everyone who believes is justified from everything you could not be justified from by the Law of Moses (Acts 13:39)

- And are justified freely by his grace through the redemp-tion that came by Christ Jesus (Rom. 3:24)
- For we maintain that a man is justified by faith apart from observing the Law (Rom. 3:28).
- Therefore, since we have been justified through faith we have peace with God through our Lord Jesus Christ (Rom. 5:1)
- And that is what some of you were. But you were washed, you were sanctified, you were justified in the name of the Lord Jesus Christ and by the Spirit of our God (1 Cor. 6:11).

SANCTIFICATION

Notwithstanding all that has just been discussed, the be-liever must make practical what has been judicially declared concerning him. If it were not necessary, then the moment he comes to faith, then he would be taken to heaven to be with the Lord, since upon become a Christian that is where his life is ... hidden with Christ in God (Col. 3:3).

But that is not the biblical model. Upon becoming a Chris-tian the believer is now called to make experiential, what he now knows to be a judicial declaration.

It is when we fail to understand this that we run the risk of confusing ourselves about who we are and what may or may not happen to us as believers. That is why Paul argues in Ro-mans 6:16 that we become slaves to that which we obey.

Clearly obedience is an act of the will, and as we saw earlier, Jesus had to learn obedience by the things He suffered. It is in obedience that we come into alignment with what God has ju-dicially declared about us and so fulfil all righteousness.

Obedience then is the defining act of the will and the divid-ing line between continuing in the former life as believers or crossing over to the life of the Spirit.

And this is why so many of the blessings already affirmed and sealed in heaven are spoken of in such conditional terms in the process of sanctification. This is the tension between those who hold to the view that once the person is truly saved he can never be eternally lost and those who hold to the view that a person truly saved, may end up lost. The challenge really seems to be understanding and appropriating two doctrines—justification and sanctification.

Justification as a judicial declaration of God is immutable. It will not and cannot change. Sanctification is the process of becoming what God has declared and as such sometimes is laced with the conditional juxtapositions. Here are a few instances:

- But now he has reconciled you by Christ's physical body through death to present you holy in his sight without blemish and free from accusation if you continue in your faith established and firm, not moved from the hope held out in the gospel (Col. 1:22, 23).
- But Christ is faithful as a son over God's household. And we are his house if we hold on to our courage and the hope of which we boast (Hebrews 3:6)
- Let us not become weary in doing good, for at the proper time we will reap a harvest, if we do not give up (Gal. 6:9).

Ostensibly, these texts are teaching conditional salvation and conditional security. We are God's house *if* we hold to our courage and our hope. We will reap the harvest *if* we do not give up and we will be presented before the throne of God, free of accusation *if* we continue in the faith.

If we think purely in terms of justification, we run the risk of embracing libertinism and if we purely think in terms of sanctification, we run the risk of legalism. Neither are we to make sanctification and extension of justification as some have tried to do, or to try to make justification an extension of sanctification as others have tried to do.

They are distinct and serve separate functions in God's scheme of things. The tension must be kept between the two, so that dangers and pitfalls may be avoided. The scriptures do not contradict themselves as some would surrender their minds to embrace, but it takes diligence and due care to observe its depth and its ultimate purpose.

Some have argued that if security and salvation were not conditional, then the texts would not even have raised them. But it seems more appropriate to the full body of scriptures to understand that there is a distinction to be made between what God declares and guarantees in justification and what He demands and requires through sanctification. Again, the two must be held in tension.

PART 2:
THE CROSS-WALK—
DYING TO LIVE

6.
THE POWER OF THE WILL

For if you live according to the sinful nature, you will die;
but if by the Spirit you put to death the misdeeds of the
body you will live (Rom. 8:13).

There is no greater arbiter to maintain the tension between
the doctrine of Justification and the doctrine of Sanctification than the human will. The most important capacity a
human being has is the ability to choose. Wars have been
fought on this one thought and thousands of lives lost in the
quest to either rob people of their right to exercise this ability
or, to preserve their right to this ability.

The capacity to choose lies in the power of the will, and the
decisions made in and by the will have fundamental and
eternal implications. If those decisions conform to the will of
God, then the person will find favour with Him, but if those
choices reject God and His will then the individual will face
His judgment and eventual loss.

There can be no downplaying the significance of the human
will. In recognition of the importance of the will and its defining role in one's ultimate outcome, the songwriter pleads, "take
my will and make it Thine, it shall be no longer mine."

GOD AND THE BELIEVER'S WILL

The believer is not a robot but even here, there is necessarily divine intervention. Paul commands the believer to work
out his salvation with reverent fear and explains that it is God
who works in the believer both to will and to do what is necessary to be done (Phil. 2:13).

What does this mean and how does God do this? Does this mean that God overrides the will of the individual that He may accomplish what He wants? Does it mean that God somehow empowers the human will that it may conform to His will or does the will too, become dead that the will of God becomes the operant force and determinant decider in the life of the believer?

From Gal. 2:19-20, Paul seems to suggest the third option. There he argues that he no longer lives and the life that he now lives is in effect the life of Christ. Is this tenuous idealism or is there something to this?

It seems that even in the surrender of the will, there is an argument to be made that the will, after the flesh, is in effect dead. That must be the heart of the argument here, for the crucifixion of the self would include the surrender of the will.

And another question would need to be raised here as well. Who or what is responsible for the first response to the will to God? In other words whose will effect the new birth?

John argues that people become children of God not by natural descent, nor by human decision, nor by husband's will but born of God (John 1:13) but he also seems to make place for "receiving" and "believing" (vs. 12). Which comes first—receiving and believing (acts of the human will) or the will of God?

Paul also argues in the same vein, saying that salvation comes by way of God's sovereign choice. Those, whom He foreknew, He predestined, called, justified, and glorified (Rom. 8:20-30).

The subject matter here is difficult and raises the universal problem of human choice and divine sovereignty. I make no pretensions at its resolution. What is clear from the scriptures is that salvation is God's idea and that those who are saved have been chosen by Him and that they have responded to Him in faith. In my view, for salvation to have the qualitative impact that God intends that it should have, then the choice of God by the individual must be one that is free, without coercion and based upon relevant spiritual information and knowledge. And yet, the gist of the scriptures is that

that none left by himself will willingly choose God (Rom. 3). Romans 9:16 says that it does not depend on man's desire or effort, but on God's mercy. It teaches that the saved are chosen in Christ before the foundation of the world according to His pleasure and His will (Eph. 1:4, 5) and 2 Timothy 3:8, 9 describes men such as Jannes and Jambres, who, as far as the faith is concerned are rejected.

Also, I have read somewhere, some long time ago that if God placed someone in heaven who did not want to be there, then heaven would become hell for that person and yet on the other side of that Paul asks in Romans 9:19—Who can resist God's will?

But back to the main point—God acts in the believer who is crucified, whose will is dead to his own capacity to choose. The believer thereby surrenders that capacity to God. In effect, the believer becomes a vessel of God. It is only as He becomes this vessel that He begins to truly live because God lives in and through him.

This is the ultimate measure of the surrender of the will. It is expressed in an understanding that the believer's decisions are no longer his to make, but God now chooses in and through him, for His glory.

If the opposite argument under the rule of the flesh is true, then the argument under the rule of God must also be true. Paul says in Romans 7 that it was no longer he who sinned, but rather it was the sin living in him (7:20). So it is under the Spirit, it may be argued that it is no longer he who does the right, but the Spirit living in him, since he has given himself over completely and totally to God.

In this regard, Paul assumes that the believer understands this and so brings into effect the answer to the prayer that Jesus taught His disciples that God's will be done on earth as it is in heaven. If that prayer is to be answered then the believer knows that it requires the crucifixion of his will as every other part of himself is crucified. Crucifixion is not complete where self-will remains alive.

SATAN AND GOD'S WILL

Satan understands this very well and encourages believers to create another will outside of the will of God. According to tradition, Lucifer got into trouble by seeking to establish that other will beyond the will of God. In popular biblical lore he is quoted as saying in his heart—

I will ascend to heaven; I will raise my throne above the stars of God, I will sit enthrone on the mount of assembly, on the utmost heights of the sacred mountain. I will ascend above the tops of the clouds; I will make myself like the most high (Is. 14:13–14).Thus began nature's rebellion against its Maker. Lucifer by seeking a will other than the will of God plunged creation into utter darkness. Some argue that the chaos found in Genesis 1 was as a direct result of the rebellion of Satan against the will of God.

The creation of another will was the creation of mutiny in the heavenly ranks and by that token Lucifer chose to become the enemy of God. His rebellion led to the seduction of Eve and plunged Adam into sin. The world has never been the same since sin, destruction and death have been the result. The will of God was challenged.

Satan became the Father of Lies because he allowed his will to deceive him and thereby created another will apart from the will of God. Any thing, any will apart from the will of God is spiritual deception.

WEAK-WILLED WOMEN (2 TIM. 3:6)

And yet as with other realities in the community of the people of God, the will is no less a challenge. In Ephesus Paul raised concern there about weak willed women being trapped by seductive false teachers. These women are ever learning, but never coming to knowledge of the truth.

From an ethical point, a brief comment must be considered here. I have not seen it developed anywhere else and so I am very cautious in presenting it. It is this. It seems that there is a diminished capacity in some to exercise the will and to that degree, moral responsibility may also be diminished.

A person whose will has been damaged such that he can only function to a limited degree in regard to the quality of the decisions he makes, regardless of how dastardly the effects of those decisions may be, must be viewed differently from someone in full control of his will and who makes the best of decisions. I do not know if the will capacity may be damaged beyond repair, but it does seem that it may be damaged to such a degree that a person might not be held totally responsible for the effect of the consequences of the capacity of the will.

Also, what is it that causes one person to be particularly disposed to a certain kind of depraved behaviour and another person with similar variables not affected by them at all? This probably belongs to the realm of ethics and psychology but one must appreciate the factors involved here.

Another point to consider in this regard is the Gethsemane encounter in which Jesus described the disciples as having willing hearts but their bodies gave way (Mark 14:32ff). They were tired and so could not do what Jesus asked them to do. This obviously is the effect of the body upon the will. Here, the will's capacity is controlled and contained in the diminished capacity of the body to respond, apparently even if it 'wanted' to.

All of this probably points to the need for the will to be surrendered, since there are so many variables which may wield some influence over it. In effect, someone may think that he is freely choosing a course of action when in fact, the will, like the conscience has already been conditioned and curtailed by the dissimilitude of the world systems, the vagaries of the sinful nature, and the seduction of demonic principalities and powers. So what a person may hold out as the exercise of his free will, may be nothing but the deceptive sounds of the unseen ventriloquist.

THE RESPONSIBILITY OF THE BELIEVER

On this issue of the will, Paul makes the point well. "Don't you know that when you offer yourselves to someone to obey him as slaves you are slaves to the one whom you obey—whether you are slaves to sin, which is death, or obedience, which leads to righteousness (Rom. 6:16)?"

For the believer, he must come to the cross and there he surrenders his will. If peace and reconciliation are to be made with God, it is required that surrender is made to Him in every detail, even in the exercise of the will.

And while the slave imagery is crass to the modern ear, it depicts well what the believer does in surrendering his will to God. The fact of the matter is this. The individual can't help but surrendering his will. In a strange accident of the strangest consequence of The Fall, the will does not become the individual's to keep, but rather the will becomes the instrument by which the individual determines whom he will serve. The will's fundamental function is to bring the person to choose not so much for himself, but critically under whose dominion he will serve. This is crucial. The biblical position concerning the will is that its use lies in determining one issue—whom shall I serve? It is as true in the Old Testament as it is in the New.

The issue of the place of service by the individual is the defining function of the will. For those who have not yet come to the cross, the options open to them are really limited. They can only choose the degree to which the will responds in favour of the world, the flesh and the devil and against God. Not so for the believer. It is he alone who is truly free to choose between what God wants and what the world, the flesh and the devil may want him to do. The unbeliever has no capacity to choose what God wants.

The scripture describes the sin nature in the individual as hostile to God. Is there a degree within the individual of the

extent of hostility? What may influence it? The sin nature cannot in any way please God but is the sin nature in every man designed the same way and hates God to the same degree? It is difficult to tell; suffice it to say that there is nothing which inheres in the sin nature within the individual which gives him a predisposition to accept God.

What God places in the individual which gives him indirect consciousness of God is the conscience. The conscience is that inner knowledge of right and wrong—that moral compass which points to a moral Law Giver, as the stars and the universe point to an all powerful Creator.

It seems then that the human will must be surrendered in the ultimate quest to be obedient to God. It probably was the most difficult test that Jesus faced, the surrender of His will. His constant theme was that He had come to do the will of His Father and that He could do nothing except what He saw His Father doing:

- Jesus gave them this answer, "I tell you the truth, the Son can do nothing by himself; he can do only what he sees his Father doing, because whatever the Father does, the son also does (John 5:19)
- By myself I can do nothing. I judge only as I hear and my judgement is just, for I seek not to please myself but him who sent me (John 5:30)
- So Jesus said, "When you have lifted up the Son of Man then you will know that I am the one I claim to be and that I do noting on my own but seek just what the Father has taught me. The one who sent me is with me; he has not left me alone, for I always do what pleases him (John 8:28, 29).

In the moment of greatest pressure, when His sweat became as great drops of blood, He asked if the cup could pass from Him, but yet, not His will, but that His Father's will be done (Matt. 26::36–46)

Going to the cross therefore means that the will must be fully and totally surrendered. Otherwise the sacrifice would be blemished and all would be lost.

7.

CRUCIFYING THE FLESH

Put to death, therefore, whatever belongs to your sinful nature: sexual immorality, impurity, lust, evil desires and greed, which is idolatry (Col. 3:5)

The scriptures clearly teach that at the death of Jesus upon the cross, several things were put to death as he died. The sinful nature or the flesh was put to death as was the world and the Law. At the cross as well, demonic principalities and powers were defeated.

The scriptures teach that all the benefits of what Jesus did in respect to the world, the law, to demonic principalities and powers and to the flesh or sinful nature accrue to the believer.

In essence the cross is the place of justification as it is the source of sanctification for the believer. But it is the aspect of sanctification with which we occupy ourselves here. This becomes vital in making our response to Him match His judicial declaration concerning us.

In that regard God sets out some clear principles concerning the flesh. The flesh is our sin nature, that capacity that we have within us to disobey God and to turn to our own way. It is that self-actualising principle within us which propels us towards life's fulfilment, without regard for true faith, even if we use religion.

There is much debate in theological circles about whether or not people are born sinners or whether they become sinners. It is not the purview of this work to explore that topic, suffice it to say that there inheres in everyone the capacity and the disposition to sin. This is the cause and the effect of the sin nature or the flesh.

The sin nature or the flesh is that within us which propels us away from God, to seek life's solutions for ourselves, without God, even if we acknowledge God and His right to be a part of our decisions. It may be outright rebellion or it may legalism. Either way, the flesh seeks to take matters in its own hand in the quest for personal fulfilment and self advancement.

Paul explains that those who live by the sin nature

- have their minds set on what the sinful nature wants (Romans 8:5)
- cannot please God (Romans 8:8)
- will die (Romans 8:13)
- He says the sinful mind
- is death (Rom. 8:6)
- is hostile to God (Rom. 8:7)
- does not submit to God's law, nor can it (Rom. 8:7)

Every person who does not have the Holy Spirit has a sinful mind, and even the believer is encouraged to renew his mind (Rom. 12:2). It is only a mind renewed by the Holy Spirit which will be able to please God in which the will of God can operate. A person who has not learnt to surrender his mind to the cross of Jesus will not be able to know the will of God.

Romans 7 gives a fulsome description of the effect of the sin nature upon an individual. Paul says that nothing good lives in his sinful nature because his sinful nature keeps on overriding the good that his conscience and the Law tell him to do. He concludes by recognising that in his sinful nature he is a slave to the law of sin. This is the cumulative effect of the sinful nature.

LEGALLY DEAD TO THE SIN NATURE

But before exploring the issue further it is important to see the judicial declaration that God makes concerning the sin nature as is done in respect to the Law, the world and demonic principalities and powers.

Romans 6:2 explains that the believer died to sin at the cross of Jesus and verse 6 explains further that we know that the old self was crucified with Him so that the body of sin might be done away with.

This crucifixion means on the one hand that the person so crucified becomes dead to all the features and the realities of the former things. The scriptures describe the believer as dead to sin, dead to the sin nature, dead to the law, dead to demonic principalities and powers and dead to the world and its systems. Apart from the Law, these represent the main features of those realities in both the spirit and the natural realm which are opposed to God and the will of God. On every count, the cross has dealt decisively with each and the believer stands as the recipient of the judicial benefit of Jesus' action on the cross.

In effect, whatever Jesus accomplished on the cross, the believer, being in Him, thereby benefits from. This is instructive. In this regard, he is dead to sin. He is dead to the sin produced by the sin nature or the flesh. The scriptures give several passages which explain what the sin nature produces:

- Put to death therefore whatever belongs to your earthly nature: sexual immorality, impurity, lust, evil desires and greed, which is idolatry... anger, rage, malice, slander and filthy language (Col. 3:5-8).
- The acts of the sinful nature are obvious: sexual immorality, impurity and debauchery; idolatry and witchcraft; hatred, discord jealousy fits of rage, selfish ambition, dissensions, faction and envy, drunkenness, orgies and the like (Gal. 5:19–21).

For the believer this is an ugly picture. As stated in Romans 6 and 7 the sin nature is in total opposition to God and the will of God. Consequently it produces in the individual every evil work imaginable.

But Paul could confidently boast, "I have been crucified with Christ and I know longer live..." (Gal. 2:20). The point is obvious.

Having been crucified with Christ, the apostle no longer lived under the dictates and the control of the sin nature. As far as he was concerned, he was dead to his sin nature and his sin nature was dead to him.

THE NEED FOR PRACTICAL SANCTIFICATION

Notwithstanding this however, the Christian has been known to fall into acts of the sin nature. In this regard, James explains that a person sins when he responds to the sin nature at work in him (James 1:13). This does not mean that sin in the life of the individual only come by way of the sin nature or the flesh, because demonic principalities and powers, the desire for the things of the world and legalism are equally strong challenges in fighting the individual to disobey God.

Things were so bad at Corinth that Paul had had to order that a man, who was sleeping with his father's wife, be removed from the fellowship (1 Cor. 5:1ff), and things were so bad at Philippi that he had to challenge the saints there to get Euodia and Syntyche to sit down and sort out their differences (Phil. 4:2), and things got so bad in Antioch that Paul publicly called Peter a hypocrite (Gal. 2:11–14).

It seems that in each case, these believers responded to the pull of the sinful nature and so plunged themselves and others in serious trouble. Paul says that such things as mark the sinful nature should not be even mentioned among the believers (Eph. 5:3) and yet these things were very present.

We have to ask ourselves, how could these things be? Is it that those who were guilty of sin did not know God and were only pretending? Is it that genuine believers were powerless against sin? Is it that believers knew their position in Christ, in terms of what has been judicially declared concerning them and so practiced a nominalism thereby continuing to flaunt their former lifestyles?

It is undoubtedly true that there will be those in the community living this way who do not know God. Paul told Corinth that there were some there who did not know God (1 Cor. 15:34) who through carnal living had demonstrated that they were acting as men devoid of the Spirit (1 Cor. 3:1-4).

But it is also true that genuine believers may fall into the trap of the sinful nature. Euodia and Syntyche were women who had their names written down in the Lamb's book of life (Phil. 4:3), so there could be very little question about the state of their salvation. But when things of this sort happen it is an indication that the believer has, by an act of the will allowed his mind to be infested by the sin nature corrupting both his body and his spirit.

The fact that some believers seem to miss is this—the position of the believer as belonging to Christ, or being owned by Christ or even being sealed and indwelt by the Holy Spirit does not guarantee true spiritual maturity. What the believer is, in his judicially declared status with God, he must make effective by willingly and obediently walking with God.

Spirituality is not so much what God has declared about the person, as elementary as that is, but rather, it is what the believer practices in his relationship with the Lord. Paul argues in several ways regarding the way that believer might find freedom from the sinful nature or the flesh.

PUT OFF THE OLD SELF (EPH. 4:20-32)

He argues that the believer is obliged to put off the old self. Remember that the old self, the old man or the sin nature or the flesh has already been crucified. However, the believer has a responsibility to put off the old self. The old self is a corrupting influence upon both body and spirit and so the believer must deliberately and consistently disassociate himself from it.

Paul wants to help the believer to see that he has a responsibility to make the distinction between the old self and the things of the Spirit. He asked in 2 Cor. 6, "Can two walk unless they agree?" That it is the point. The believer cannot expect to keep on walking carrying both the old man and the new man in the same vessel. Paul describes this in 2 Cor. 7:1 as corruption of both body and spirit.

The more corrupted the spirit of the believer becomes, the more susceptible he becomes to the other enemies that he faces—the world and demons. It is very important that spiritual care-givers become aware of the entrance points to sin in the lives of believers. Everything does not come by way of the flesh or the sin nature and everything does not come by way of the seduction of the world. Nor does everything come by way of demons. Spiritual care-givers need to be aware so that the right remedy can be applied. It calls for spiritual maturity and discerning.

Here Paul points to the destructiveness of the old self. The old self is like a plant which springs up very easily even after being cut down and so constant vigilance is required. In a sense, even though it has been crucified at the cross, it has not been gotten rid of. Paul calls the believer to put it off, because left where it is, it will grow again.

PUT TO DEATH (COL. 3:5)

Another way that Paul describes what needs to be done is that the believer is to put to death the things of the earthly nature. This is the decisive action that Jesus addresses in the Sermon on the Mount. If your eye offends, pluck it out, and if your hand offends, cut it off.

The crucified life requires this kind of decisive action. It is war. Obviously, Jesus was not teaching self-mutilation. He was making the point that the believer who would live for God must be committed to removing the offence of the flesh from his life.

The crucified life knows the horror of sin and will have an unparalleled hatred for it. Sin is natural in the believer's breast by way of the sin nature. He must cultivate a holy hatred for it and be willing to cut it out wherever he finds it in himself. There is no place here for negotiation. There is no place here for gradual withdrawal. The action must be decisive. The thing must be killed.

The offences of the flesh stand in constant opposition and war against the will of God. In fact, Paul writes in Galatians 5 that the reason why the believer cannot do what he wants to do is because of the war between the Spirit and the sin nature.

It is very short-sighted to see spiritual warfare only in terms of fighting demons. The Galatians text points to the fact that there is war between the flesh and the Spirit. This almost sounds incredulous. How can the Spirit of God be fighting the sin nature?

We must understand that in the doctrine of justification God acts alone, but in the doctrine of sanctification, He invites us to cooperate with Him through the Holy Spirit and to act as He would act. He invests in us the capacity to make the decisions the way He would make them. But in sanctification we must make them. He won't make decisions for us that He has already delegated to us to take responsibility for.

The Holy Spirit is thereby constrained by the decisions that we make. That is why we may grieve Him (Eph. 4:30). He is constrained in the process of sanctification by our decisions. And that is why we may quench Him (1 Thes. 5:19). In certain things, God permits Himself to be bound by our decisions. In the former, our moral decisions may bring sadness and pain to Him and in the latter our ministry decisions may not take Him into account.

CLOTHE YOURSELF (COL. 3:12)

Too often, Christian action does not go far enough. We fail to see the interconnectedness of spiritual realities and do not follow through all the way in treating with the problems and the sins which so easily beset us. The crucified life calls for complete action.

In 1 Samuel 15, God tells Saul to get rid of the Amelekites. He was to totally destroy everything—men, women, children and livestock. Saul gathered the fighting men. On the way, he met the Kenites. He instructed them to get out of the way which they did. God's words were that the Amelekites should be destroyed.

He went to fight the Amelekites and did a God ordered except that he saved the good things—the king, fatted calves, and lambs. The text says that they were unwilling to destroy completely the things that God had told them to. They brought these good things back home.

But God was not pleased. God was grieved that He had made Saul king. The prophet confronted the king. The king explained that he had carried out the Lord's instructions, blessing the prophet in the process. He could not see the folly of his ways. When confronted about the sheep and the other animals Saul explained that the reason why he had saved the good things was because the soldiers wanted to use the best of what the Amelekites had to make a sacrifice to the Lord.

The prophet was livid. What God wanted from the King was not what he thought he should give Him. He wanted full obedience. One may be tempted to think that God could have been easy on Saul. After all, he saved the animals to make a sacrifice to the Lord. But Saul missed the point. God wanted obedience.

So it is too at the cross The crucified life is about absolute obedience. Contrary to the popular notion that "He is not Lord at all if he is not Lord of all" He remains Lord even in our unfaithfulness, for He cannot deny Himself. The crucified life requires shedding of all that we are and have but it also requires our taking upon ourselves all that Christ is. It is only complete when we have taken Christ at the cross, not only surrender our selves there.

We must come to the cross, where we find God's declaration concerning the sin nature, fully and absolutely dealt with. But there must be the exercise of our will in which we are manifestly seen to be participating with God to make what He has declared over us our joyful experience.

8.
CRUCIFYING THE WORLD

May I never boast except in the cross of our Lord Jesus Christ through which the world has been crucified to me and I to the world (Gal. 6:14)

The Scriptures teach that the believer must continue to live in the world. He must function in the world, obey its leaders, conform to its laws and so on. And yet the believer must resist the world. It is a tension that the believer dare not ignore. He is an ambassador from another place and so the point of reference for living is from another place.

Here again the Apostle identifies what is clearly the believer's position in Christ. He has been crucified to the world and the world has been crucified to him. What he now enjoys is the new creation described in 2 Cor.5:17.

In Col. 2:20 Paul says the same thing another way—Since you died with Christ to the basic principles of this world, why as though you still belonged to it do you still submit to its rules...?

The person who is in Christ died to the rules and principles of the world. He had to, or he cannot walk in the power of the Spirit. The believer through crucifixion surrenders himself up to kingdom living by dying to the world and worldly living.

Jesus said to the disciples in John 16:33, "Take heart, I have overcome the world."

And John also describes the believer as someone who has already overcome the world. He says—for everyone born of God overcomes the world, even your faith. Who is it that overcomes the world? Only he who believes that Jesus is the Son of God (1 John 5:4, 5)

The believer then, stands in the place of one who has total mastery over the ways of the world. He is in effect beyond its gravitational pull. He lives in the context of being undisturbed by the spiritual pull of the world. It has no power over him.

These are some of the truths that the scriptures record about the world:

- the world does not know the Spirit, Jesus, the Father, nor the believers (John 1:10, 14:17, 17:25; 1 John 3:1)
- The kingdom of Jesus does not belong to this world (John 18:36)
- In a day to come, Jesus will judge the world (Acts 17:31)
- Whoever is a friend of the world is an enemy of God (James 4:4)
- The world hates the believers (John 15:18, 17:14; 1 John 3:13).
- The whole world is under the control of the evil one (1 John 5:19; John 12:31, 14:30, 16:11; 2 Cor. 4:4)

Every believer ought to take these facts very seriously. Also, it must be borne in mind that worldliness does not only have to do with morally reprehensible behaviour. Jesus described the synagogues and the Temple as belonging to the world (John 18:20).

As an ambassador, the believer's point of reference for life and meaning is not as things obtains in the world, but his point of reference is now the principles and the rule set in heaven.

This is why there must be this tension within the believer as he seeks to live in the world. He knows that he does not belong to it, and yet the world uses all kinds of strategies to get the believer to conform to what it sets out.

The system of the world is treacherous and opposed to anything that God wills. Its peace is fleeting and tentative, its education is self serving, its quest for unity is self-serving, and its policies as tenuous as they are serve another god.

Worldliness is antithetical to holiness and true spirituality. It may parade in the guise of spirituality, but without the cross, such a spirituality has no binding centre and without a binding centre men are lost.

So at the cross, the believer dies to the world, its lures and its attractions. He is the holder of diplomatic immunity from the world and all its charges set against him.

LIVING APART FROM THE WORLD

And yet the scriptures clearly point to at least one believer who allowed himself to fall for the world. Paul, in his last moments was deserted by most of those who were closest to him. In 2 Tim. 3:6, he talks about being poured out like a drink offering and that it was time for him to die. He describes the confidence he has in seeing God upon his departure.

He then turns to the tight emotional corner that he faced, encouraging young Timothy to come to him quickly and to bring Mark with him. Then he drops the bombshell, as it were —Demas, because he loved this world has deserted me and has gone to Thessalonica (9). Can you imagine how young Timothy must have felt at the news of Demas' departure?

Paul may be describing that event when he wrote in verse 16, "At my first defence, no one came to my support, but everyone deserted me." In the face of the hostility of the world to the message, Demas retreated to the world. He could not take the pressure. But Paul had earlier written in 2 Tim 1:11-12, And of this gospel, I was appointed a herald and an apostle and a teacher. That is why I am suffering as I am. Yet, I am not ashamed, because I know whom I have believed and am convinced that he is able to guard what I have entrusted to him for that day.

The suffering that the apostle encountered was in acknowledgement that he was no longer following the world. The one who had persecuted the church most vigorously and ferociously had become its staunchest defender and missionary protagonist. Paul explains that Alexander the metal worker did him much harm, and warned Timothy to be on the guard against him (14–15). This man may have frightened Demas to such an extent that he returned to the things and the ways of the world.

You will recall that this Demas was the same one who accompanied the apostle on his journeys. In both Colossians (4:13) and Philemon (24) he is identified with Paul sending greetings to the churches while Paul was in prison, and in the latter text, he is described there as a fellow worker along with Mark, Aristarchus and Luke.

Demas fell in love with the world and deserted the apostle probably when he needed him most. His new friendship with the world overtook his commitment to the apostle and the principles of the kingdom.

The crucified life proved too demanding for Demas and so he succumbed to the drag of the former way of things. Like the flesh, the world produces the same kinds of results in the individual who follow its ideas and philosophies.

WORLDLINESS REFUSES TO RETAIN THE KNOWLEDGE OF GOD

At its core, worldliness is refusing to retain the knowledge of God in one's thinking. When the psalmist writes, "the fool says in his heart, there is no God", he is not making an atheist of the fool. On the contrary, he is pointing to the moral depravity of those who seek to live their lives without God. They disregard God's character and the righteous demands that He makes are thrown out the window. The morally depraved would rather appeal to 'humanness' and human reason over God's revelation for right action. Paul describes it in Romans 1:28–32.

Furthermore, since they did not think it worthwhile to retain the knowledge of God, he gave them over to a depraved mind, to do what ought not to be done. They have become filled with every kind of wickedness, evil, greed and depravity. They are full of envy, murder strife, deceit and malice. They are gossips and slanderers God haters, insolent arrogant and boastful;

they invent ways of doing evil, they disobey their parents; they are senseless, faithless, heartless, ruthless, Although they know God's righteous decree that those who do such things deserve death, they not only continue to do these things but also approve of those who practice them.

This is a long list, but worldliness is seen in these things in the way that acts of the flesh are to be seen in similar things. While acts of the flesh may be said to be driven from within, what motivates the individual to respond to these horrid acts is the mental frame that he takes to God and the lure of the systems of the world.

The sin nature or the flesh appeals from within, the world appeals from without, even though they offer similar attractions. The sin nature appeals to the soul while the world appeals to the body.

John writes of it in 1 John 2:15-17. He warns the believer against loving the world and concludes that anyone who loves the world does not have the love of God in him. It is a hard word, but a true word. There are three things that mark a love of the world:self-indulgence, lustful dissatisfaction and self-congratulation.

THE BELIEVER'S RESPONSE

Crucifying the world requires surrendering all three which come easily and naturally to the individually, but which must never be known in the community of the new creation.

Paul explains that the way to deal with the world is by way of being transformed by the renewing the mind (Rom. 12:1, 2). And so, here again is the believer's responsibility in light of what he has been called to. The response to the world for the believer requires a concentrated mind, a mind aimed at discovering and appropriating the will of God.

When the believer concentrates his mind on knowing and fulfilling God's will then his mind will begin to occupy itself with the principles of the new creation, but when it flirts with the philosophies and the ideas of the world, then he will begin to court those principles which are directly opposed to God.

In 2 Cor. 1:12–14 Paul also discusses how he conducted himself in the world. He said that their conduct was marked by holiness, sincerity and the grace of God. These three characteristics must mark believers as they live in the world and interact with it.

To Be or Not To Be

It is very easy to understand why some Christians run away from the world in seclusion in the hope of keeping themselves from contamination by the world. It is also very easy to understand too why some Christians eagerly "want to go to heaven and rest."

But Jesus' prayer was never that we should be taken out of this world, or that we should desire to go to heaven and rest. He taught His disciples to pray, "let your kingdom come." It is a most politically subversive prayer, for this prayer is asking for the overthrow and the removal of things in the world, the way they are. The prayer for the coming of the kingdom emphasises the fact that the kingdoms of the world are only temporary and the eventual solution is not that we leave the world, but that the world be subsumed in the kingdom of God, not as it is, but changed and transformed.

The work of the believer in this regard is critical. His mind must be geared towards discovering the will of God and causing that will to have influence in the world. The world knows this and so it either tries to destroy those Christians who understand and are practising it, or it lulls Christians into a type of reasonable compromise, a kind of truce.

So the response of those who want to be taken out of the world betrays a sad and regrettable attitude for Jesus' prayer is not that they be taken out of the world but that in the face of the hatred of the world, they would be protected from the evil one, the god of this world (John 17:15).

So while departing this world may be more attractive as Paul argues, it is more needful that the believer stays in the world (Phil. 1:21–26). In the conversation that Paul had with himself he said that he did not know which to chose, whether to be with the Philippian believers or to go and to be with the Lord.

Paul's spiritual principle in this discussion is clear. The needful must be chosen over the better in the question of whether one should go and be with the Lord or stay in the world that the kingdom of God might advance in it. He says that he would continue with the Philippians 'for their progress and joy in the faith...' (1:25).

In respect to the world, the crucified life understands that the option is not running away from it, rather, it is being dead to its influence, not facing it in the energy of the flesh, but in the power of the Holy Spirit.

The believer is never at liberty to 'monasticise' himself from the world. He is the world's salt and light and he is the fragrance of Christ. He must remain in the world to be all that God wants him to be.

As light, he gives hope, direction, meaning and clarity to life. As light he dispels and expels the darkness. He brings new perspectives to things as people shed the ways of the world and are given a new understanding of living.

As salt, he preserves the world from corruption; he adds real flavour to the dullness of life. Truly it is only the believer who knows how to enjoy life.

And as the fragrance of Christ (2 Cor. 2:14) he reveals spiritual things to a world deceived by its blind spots, its self-importance and its own needs. The woman poured out a whole alabaster box of ointment upon the head of Jesus. Some understood it and was saved. Others grumbled and were lost.

Believers need to know that the world is fundamentally hostile to the cross. It should not come as surprise that the world should respond that way to Christians. Jesus spends time in prayer on this very point as He prayed in John 17.

9.

VICTORY OVER LEGALISM
AND THE LAW

He forgave us all our sins, having cancelled the written code, with its regulations that was against us and that stood opposed to us; he took it away nailing it to the cross (Col. 2:13, 14).

One of the most dangerous traps the person in the church has to contend with is the trap of legalism. Simply put, legalism is obedience to the Word of God with no spiritual connection to God. A classic example is to be found in those who hold the moral value of the scriptures in high regard and practise them, but who have no real relationship with God.

Many of them are trapped in their various traditions and religious mores trying to please God through effort and explanation rather than through surrender. Traditions are not bad in themselves, but they become traps of legalism when the traditions give way to traditionalism—the unbending desire and the unyielding will to keep ideas, practices and structures which oppose God's revelation.

Laws call us to do things to be in good standing. The challenge is that individuals may be tempted to do things to find approval with the Law. And this is the danger, approval is sought of the Law, but not of the Law Giver. Legalism occurs when the practice of the Law becomes more important than a relationship with the Law Giver.

The Christian is called to a Person, not to laws and rules. His obedience and allegiance is to a Person, not to the rules themselves. It is a subtle but importance difference. That is why

Paul could argue for instance, that the promise made could not be annulled by the law given.

But to say that the Christian is called to a Person and not to rules is not to say that the kingdom has no rules. What is to be kept in mind at all times is the need to focus on building relationship with the Person, not just being obedient to laws without understanding the divine connection.

The text quoted above describes the written code. In the discussion on the believer as a part of the new creation, it was observed there that the written code is in fact the written law. Paul explains in different places what the Law is and what it was intended to do.

The ministry that brought death engraved in letters on stone (2 Cor. 3:7). The Law, even though it served as the basic (moral) principle of the world served to bring death. Its effect was to remind people of their powerlessness in the face of a holy God and the impossibility of living for Him. In effect, the law served to place persons in a moral and spiritual prison.

Through the Law we become conscious of sin (Rom. 3:20) Paul explains that sin-consciousness is created by the Law. If no Law were given, then there would be no knowledge of sin. In the Law the conscience is awakened to the fact of sinfulness, because it is through the command that the individual is made aware that he has missed the mark of God.

Law brings wrath (Rom. 4:15). In that regard therefore, the Law has served to help men to see that they are under God's wrath. From the first Adam until Christ, the effect of the Law was to place men under condemnation. It is in Christ, the second Adam, that the wrath of God passes.

The Law was added so that the Trespass might increase (Rom. 5:20) There is something strange and paradoxical about a knowledge of laws. Contrary to the popular notion that information will lead to transformation, the very opposite might equally happen. It is those who know what the rule says who sometimes flaunt it the most, especially if they feel that it is repressive.

You died to the Law through the body of Christ (7:4) Romans also teaches that in the death of Christ, the believer died to the Law. Again, this is his true position in Christ. The Law has no right nor hold over him. He is released from any relationship to the Law.

Apart from law, sin is dead (Rom. 7:8) One of the reasons why no record of sins is kept against the believer is because of this very fact. The Law which insists on record keeping has been abrogated and the records expunged. As a result, there can be no censure or judgement for those who are in Christ Jesus.

The very commandment that was intended to bring life brought death (7:10) This has been repeated again and again in the scriptures. While its theological range may difficult to grasp, its core message is true. Instead of imparting life, the commandment brought death. Paul makes the point that if the Law could have imparted life, then Jesus would not have died.

The Law is holy and the commandment is holy righteous and good (7:12) But this is not to be disparaging of the Law. It would be sinful to do that. The Laws were given by a holy God to direct the natural order. But that which is holy given to unholy men will soon be trampled by them. He sent His Son He was trample under the feet of men. So in effect, the Law stands as a testimony against the corruptness of the human heart, because the heart is desperately wicked.

The Law is spiritual (7:14) This is a spiritual principle function-
ing in a natural world. The effect would be obvious. This
spiritual principle as holy as it is cannot produce in natural
men, what God intends. The effect is that the Law as a spiritual reality cannot show what is good in men, but rather
what he is incapable of. In effect, the Law condemns men,
because it is spiritual and men are natural, spiritually dead
and unable to bear it.

By observing the Law, no one can be justified (Gal. 2:16). Some
have argued for the necessity of observing the Law for justification. In other words, justification is contingent upon
obedience to the Law. This position makes a mockery of the
gift of God in justification, because justification is the legally
completed work of Jesus credited to the believer through
faith. It is never contingent upon effort. Any attempt to gain
God's favour by human effort becomes legalism. Legalism
was nailed to the cross.

And again, to argue that the person so justified must also
turn around to obey the Law to either find or to maintain justification misses a fundamental theological point, because
the act of God's justifying the sinner can in no way be now
married to man's effort to please Him. Such a thing leads
only to boasting, and this is why so many church groups are
arrogant about their beliefs. They have forgotten that the Law
and justification are mutually exclusive concepts.

Through the Law, I died to the Law (2:19) The Law is the ministry of death and by it, no one shall find life. It is holy, just
and good. However as a source of life it fails decisively. Its
best capacity is to remind conscience of man's miserable
failure before God. The letter kills.

Righteousness cannot be Gained through the Law (2:21) As discussed under the theme of not being able to be justified by
the Law, this text makes a similar point.

All who rely on observing the Law are under a curse (3:10) This is a fundamental point, not to be missed. Everyone who insists on keeping the Law will admit that they are doing so to please God. It simply cannot be done and the consequence is God's displeasure.

The Law is not based on faith (3:12) This point necessarily follows, because the Law is based on what men can do. Law requires no faith. And faith is the bedrock of true salvation.

The Law was added because of transgression (3:19) Human transgression preceded the giving of the Law. To show the awful horror of sin, God gave the Law to make known how utterly horrible transgression really is.

We were held prisoners by the Law until faith should be revealed (3:23) The revelation of faith now abrogates the Law. It is not that faith now makes Law observance possible. The coming of faith rearranges the covenants once again. For the Law must now give way to faith, since Law and faith cannot co-exist.

We no longer need the supervision of the Law (3:25) The terms used to describe the Law here are most telling. The Law was a supervisor. Above, the Law was a jailer. None of these terms now fit the arrangement that the new community now shares with God

To turn back to the Law is to turn back to weak and beggarly elements (4:9) This is an exceedingly strong argument from the apostle. To go back to the Law is to go back to feeble and fragile elements. This is the danger that many groups fall into. They want to hold the gift of God in one hand and the ministry of works in the other. The Law is simply not based on faith and so, it is weak and beggarly. To try to serve the

Law and to walk in faith is a corruption of true spiritually because the one requires sight and the other does not.

The Promise and the Law cannot co-exist (4: 21–31). This follows on the point just made above. You cannot be seeing and trusting at the same time. Paul argues that if you see what you hope for, then such a hope is meaningless. Those who seek to live by the Law are living by what they see. Those who live by Christ are seeing *through* the One they have come to believe in. It makes a critical difference to how one lives his life.

The Law is a Yoke of Slavery (5:1) Paul repeats the theme of the Law being a yoke of slavery. He anticipates the accusation of libertinism here as he does in Romans. He says, "You my brothers were called to be free. But do not use your freedom to indulge the sinful nature, but rather serve one another in love" (Gal. 5:15) and in Romans 3:8 Paul addresses those who were arguing that he was encouraging libertinism by this teaching. To break the yoke of the slavery of the Law does not mean that a person is now disposed to do anything. On the contrary Paul argues that such a person is now "in-lawed" to Christ (1 Cor. 9:21).

Even Peter weighs in on the discussion. He argues that our freedom from the yoke of slavery should not be used as a cloak for unrighteous living, but the empowerment to truly serve one another (1 Pet. 2:16).

Those who try to be justified by the Law are alienated from Christ (5:4) There is no life in those who seek justification before God by obeying the Law. This is a difficult thing to admit, but it remains true, and this does not only apply to the attempt to keep Jewish Law, but also the laws and traditions of churches and groups designed to gain favour with God.

Favour with God is always an act of God's grace. He has mercy on whomever He wishes to have mercy. Legalism always wants to contribute to gaining God's favour. Legalism only leads to alienation from God as the Pharisees, the ones who sat in the seat of Moses were to find out.

All of the above indicate to us the place of the Law. The subtlety lies always in seeking even by way of biblical commands to find relationship with God without going the right way.

The Law is not based on faith. The crucified life is the starting point of faith. That is why trying to please God by any other means except trusting Him corrupts the crucified life.

The surrender that God calls for is an absolute surrender. Its scandal is in its simplicity. It is foolishness to some and a stumbling block to others because there is the inner ignorance and the outer arrogance of being unable to apprehend and to appropriate what God has done in Christ Jesus.

Obeying the rules and laws must be surrendered so that the Christ life may be born in us. Personal morality has no place in the Christ life, what matters is a moral code framed in the Spirit which is now written upon a new heart.

The Old Code with all its similarities to the requirements to the New Covenant principles is fundamentally different from the New Creation principles. It is not only that the principles are "elevated"—written in the hearts rather than upon stone—but the principles form the context of a living relationship already guaranteed.

These new principles are given to spiritually alive people, with the capacity to respond to God, not given to a world of death and decay pointing people to damnation. Under the world, the Law was a witness to death and the decaying order. In the new spiritual order the principles are given celebrating the freedom that is to be found in God.

10.

VICTORY OVER POWERS AND AUTHORITIES

And having disarmed the powers and authorities he made a public spectacle of them, triumphing over them by the cross (Col. 2:15).

One of the most controversial areas of Christian living is in the area of the Christian's response to demons. What is the extent of demonic influence upon Christians? Can Christians be demonised, in the sense of being occupied by demons or do demons only exert external influence to the same effect as if they were demonised?

There are good arguments on both sides of the discussion and it is not the purview of this brief work to delve into that topic, suffice to say that as the key determinant by the believer to the world and to the sin nature is his will, so it is with his response to demonic principalities and powers.

As with the sin nature, the world, and the Law, demonic principalities and powers were also treated with at the cross. Indeed, Jesus came to destroy the works of the devil (I John 3:8).

What do Demons do?

These beings are very, very active. The scriptures identify their activities in several places.

- Jesus describes Satan as coming to steal, to kill and to destroy (John 10:10)
- Satan masquerades as an angel of light seeking to deceive people (2 Cor. 11:14)

- The Devil traps, captures and enslaves people to do his will (2 Tim. 2:26)
- Satan prowls around like a roaring lion seeking to devour whom he may (2 Pet. 5:8)
- Satan causes people to lie, since he is the father of lies (John 8:44)
- Demons possess people causing them to become physically sick, emotionally sick and spiritually sick.
- The boy who appeared epileptic was in fact under demonic occupation
- The daughter of the Syro-Phoenician woman who appeared physically sick was in fact demon possessed
- The woman who was physically bent over for eighteen years was in fact bound by Satan
- The man who lived in the tombs who seemed to have had a mental breakdown was in fact demon possessed
- Some of the religious leaders of Jesus' day were described as *belonging* to their father the devil, not only showing demonic influence and control of the religious system, more seriously, owning these individuals.

THE BELIEVER'S LEGAL STANDING

The Scriptures are clear. In Jesus Christ, the Prince of the world is driven out (John 8:31). John 16:11 continues the theme that in the cross, Satan stood condemned. So from very early, Jesus speaks confidently about His victory over Satan. The writer of Hebrews 2:14 says, that Jesus by His death destroyed the devil who held the power of death and freed those who lived all their lives in fear of death.

That victory has been the privilege of every believer. What Jesus effected on the cross concerning Satan and His demons is the heritage of every child of God.

·   ·   ·   ·   ·

More than a Conqueror (Rom. 8:37)

In that regard, the scriptures teach that demons cannot separate the child of God from the love of God (Rom. 8:37). He [Satan] tried to separate Adam and Eve from God by accusing God before them and he tried to separate God from Job by accusing Job before God. In both instances the plot backfired, since he lost on both counts. His plot against Adam brought the full might of heaven into the natural world and his plot against Job left Job in a better position that he was before he (Satan) ever opened his mouth.

In a second regard, the believer as a member of the body of Christ is a conqueror in that all that Satan intended against him was dealt with in Jesus' own triumph over him at the cross. And so the scriptures teach that the believer has not been given a spirit of fear, but one of love, power and self control (2 Tim. 1:7).

It teaches that the believer has not been made a slave again to fear, but he has received the spirit of sonship, whereby he is affirmed in his state as a son of God and joint heir with Jesus (Rom. 8:15–17).

A third regard in which the believer is a conqueror lies in Jesus' declaration concerning the church. He says that the gates of hell would not prevail against it. To prevail means to triumph over or to succeed against. In that usage the gates of hell is powerless against the church (Matt. 16:18-19).

This leaves hell vulnerable to the church, not the church vulnerable to hell. It means that the church has the authority to go against the bastions of hell, release its captives without fear of loss.

And so, the idea of the believer as more than a conqueror reinforces the victory and the dominance that he has over everything and everyone demonic and diabolical.

. . . . .

THE BELIEVER CANNOT BE HARMED BY THE EVIL ONE (1 JOHN 5:18)

Here again the scriptures declare the believer beyond demonic reach. Jesus judged and condemned Satan at the cross. He has no legal right to anyone, having faced the full blast of the judgement of God (John 16:11). In the judgment of God, demonic principalities and powers had the sentence of death passed upon them and they only await final sentencing. As beings living under God's judgment, they are powerless against those living in the light and the power of an Almighty God.

PRACTICAL CONSIDERATIONS

And yet, believers are in constant danger of demonic destruction. Jesus taught that the thief comes to steal, to kill and to destroy (John 10:10). When God asked Stan where he was coming from he told God that he is coming from walking through the world, going up and down in it. Even though he has been defeated and judgement has been passed upon him, Satan remains the god of this world.

It is absolutely true that his operation has been rendered powerless by the act of the cross. What the believer must constantly be mindful of is that demonic principalities and powers are still a part of the spiritual landscape. The traps that he set are still in effect—like minefields left after a war—and his own attitude remains one of defiance, refusing to acknowledge the sovereign rule of the Lord Jesus Christ.

The devil knows that he has been defeated. He knows that judgment has been passed upon him, but he has not yet bowed to Jesus. Paul reminds the Christians that the day will come when every knee will bow and every tongue will confess that Jesus Christ is Lord to the glory of God.

·   ·   ·   ·   ·

LIKE ROARING LION (1 PET. 5:8)

Peter describes him as a roaring lion, prowling around, seeking whom he may devour. There is an apt description of this in Psalm 22, 16–21.

Dogs have surrounded me; a band of evil men has encircled me. They have pierced my hands and my feet... Deliver my life from the sword, my precious life from the power of the dogs. Rescue me from the mouth of the lions; save me from the horns of the wild oxen.

This is an apt description of demonic activity against the people of God. In that regard, Peter argues that believers need to be vigilant. There is the popular maxim in some circles that if you don't interfere with demonic principalities and powers they won't interfere with you. This is at best naïve. Jesus spent probably up to a third of His ministry dealing with and teaching about demons. And in his very short letter 1 John, the apostle spent quite a deal of time talking about demons as well. Look at what John has to say about demonic principalities and powers in this letter which one might have thought should avoid the subject altogether:

- He reminds the believers that they have overcome the evil one (2:13–14)
- Those who continue to practise sin belong to the devil (3:8)
- The devil has been sinning from the beginning (3:8)
- Jesus appeared to destroy the works of the devil (3:8)
- Anyone who does not do what is right, or who does not love his brother remains a child of the devil (3:10)
- The evil one instigated the murder of Abel by Cain (3:12)
- Spirits are to be tested and those which deny that Jesus is from God are to be rejected. (4: 1–3)
- The evil one cannot harm those born of God (5:18)
- The whole world is under the control of the evil one (5:19)

Clearly, what is needed is not over-occupation about demonic principalities and powers but a proper knowledge of what the Word teaches and what course of action is to be taken. There is no bliss in ignorance here. Demonic principalities and powers are on the prowl after believers whether believers are paying attention or not. The believer needs to take the Petrine warning very, very seriously. The adversary is prowling around looking for someone to eat alive.

SATAN PREVENTED US (1 THESS. 2:18)

Here again is the demonic activity against the people of God and the work of God. Paul says here that he repeatedly wanted to visit the Thessalonians but Satan stopped him. This does not mean that Paul had somehow become powerless against Satan, but what it ought to highlight for the believer is the awareness that Satan may and will intervene in the plans and affairs of the people of God to disrupt and to set back the work.

A MESSENGER OF SATAN (2 COR. 12:7)

This was discussed earlier in the context of the suffering of the believer. But I am highlighting it here to make the point that though the scriptures teach the principle that Satan cannot touch the believer, here Satan has a big part to play in Paul's fourteen year thorn in the flesh. It was described as a messenger of Satan designed by him and sent to torment Paul.

THE ACCUSER OF THE BRETHREN (REV. 12:10)

John describes Satan as the accuser of the believers. How he gets to stand in the heavenly courts to carry out this activity remains a mystery. But we saw a glimpse of this in the story of Job and in the story of the high priest Joshua in Zechariah 3.

The word Satan means accuser and as such he finds every means by which he accuses believers to their faces, he accuses believers to each other and he even goes to the throne room of heaven daily to accuse believers. Evidently, at this last accusation in Revelation 12, he is finally and permanently denied access and thrown out of heaven.

SATAN FILLED ANANIAS' HEART (ACTS 5:3)

In this most telling case, Ananias and Sapphira allowed themselves to be seduced by Satan so much so that they lied to the Holy Spirit, upon the devil's instigation. Now it is quite possible that lying may be as a direct consequence of the operation of the sin nature, but here, such is not the case. The source of this horrendous act was none other than the father of lies, himself.

Satan is described here as filling Ananias' heart in the same way the believer is admonished to be filled with the Holy Spirit (Eph. 5:18). Whatever else may be gleaned from this text, it is abundantly clear that demonic activity is very strong in the world and against the believer in particular and he needs to be aware of the traps and the dangers.

DO NOT BE UNAWARE OF HIS DEVICES (2 COR. 2:11)

Knowing demonic devices is an important responsibility of the believer. It is among the ways that the believer will avoid being outwitted or being taken advantage of by the devil. The crucified life requires the believer to be ahead of the devil in all his plans and strategies. It is when there is lapse into complacency, ignorance or arrogance that trouble begins. Hosea laments this very point that the people are destroyed because of their ignorance (Hosea 4:6).

The first thing to accept in this regard is the fact that God wants the community and the believers to be aware of the demonic realm. It is among the safeguards and to neglect the safeguard is to create problems for the people of God.

SUBMIT TO GOD AND RESIST THE DEVIL (JAMES 4:7)

Here James is setting things in order. The believer must continue to act responsibly. He is making the point that where there is not a submissive spirit then the avenue is made open for demonic defeat. He begins chapter 4 by pointing to the dangers of fighting the wrong battles—other believers.

He is making the point that fighting each other indicates inner individual turmoil. He argues that this inner turmoil is also indicative of selfishness and materialism—sure signs of a haughty spirit.

He then argues that what is needed is submission to God, living close to Him, resisting the devil and in that context, he will flee. Clearly resisting the devil by itself will not guarantee victory over him. In this context there needs to be a spirit of submission, nearness to God, and a holy hatred of sin.

RESIST HIM, STANDING FIRM IN THE FAITH (1 PETER 5:9)

Across the scriptures, the point is clear. Positional truths by themselves do not guarantee personal success. It is when the believer actively seeks to make what God has declared legally about him real, that life's experiences take on new meaning and broader dimensions.

Peter adds another dimension to the need to resist the devil. If the believer had simply settled on what God had declared concerning him, without striving to practise what God has said about him, then his life would be compromised and God's Word would be held to public ridicule.

In this text, the chapter again begins with the issue of humility. Elders are to be humble, young men are to be humble and this is to be marked by the willingness to submit.

In light of that, the believer is to be self controlled and alert. To be alert implies being ready to act and to be attentive. He is not to let his guard down. Serious commitment to prevent the devil from touching the believer is required from the believer.

He is required to stand firm in the faith as he resists the devil, but this must be done in a context of humility, self control and the readiness to fight.

GIVING THE DEVIL A PLACE (EPH. 4:27)

Here Paul warns the believer not to give the devil a foothold. Footholds become strongholds when believers do not heed the Word. The Holy Spirit is grieved (Eph. 4:30) when believers allow the foothold to the devil.

The idea of the foothold is in fact a military concept which points to the surrender of ground to the enemy. When this happens the enemy will take whatever course of action which will not only preserve that space, but will seek to extend it.

HAVE NOTHING TO DO WITH THE DEEDS OF DARKNESS (EPH. 5:11)

The believer is also warned to avoid secret, dark things. We have seen how strong the believer's position is in God. But Paul calls Timothy to take care about entanglement. He says to him that no soldier who is serving in the army gets entangled in civilian affairs. It is in this sense that the believer must learn to make distinctions.

Obviously as the text further reveals, it calls for wisdom, because the days are evil and nothing can be taken for granted. So while one might truly rejoice and rightly so that the evil one cannot touch him, that he is more than a conqueror, that he is no longer under the ownership of the devil and so on, he must be fully aware that these things in themselves, as important as they are do not guarantee that he himself will be safe, if he does not take seriously the preventative and proactive action necessary to make meaningful and satisfying what God judicially declared concerning him.

CRUSHING THE SERPENT UNDERFOOT (ROM. 16:20)

To read a verse like this almost gives the impression that the work at Calvary was somehow incomplete. Paul suggests that Satan's head would soon be crushed under the feet of the believers. What the text is in fact acknowledging is that the judged enemy has not yet bowed. It points to the carrying out of the sentence against him which is still to come. Until then, the believer must know that special care is to be taken in how he treats with and responds to the demonic world.

TRENDS

In conclusion, look carefully at the trend among believers in the scriptures, despite what God declared them to be. In respect to the responding to the flesh, Paul reports that there was a believer sleeping with his father's wife. This had nothing to do with demons or the world per se. He was responding to his sinful nature. Euodia and Syntyche were having serious problems in Philippi, which required public admonition.

Look also at the story of Demas. Despite what God had judicially declared about the believer concerning the world, we read of Demas going back to the world. The judicial declaration was not immunity for the believer to act contrary to what God had said about him.

In respect to legalism, the whole church of Galatia was in danger of returning to it. In fact even Peter and Barnabas became trapped in this dreadful sin.

And finally in respect to demons Ananias and his wife succumbed to them and lied to the Holy Spirit. Ananias is described as allowing Satan "to fill his heart," a term that you would rightly expect to be limited to the work of the Holy Spirit. But as it is, instead of the Holy Spirit, it was demons filling his heart.

Again, I want to make the point that being in Christ does not guarantee personal and practical immunity from the world, the flesh, principalities and powers or from legalism. Being in Christ does not guarantee spirituality. There is no place for repose, but a constant and unrelenting watch to guard against these enemies of the soul.

The true guarantee is to be found in a life of surrender, full, total and unequivocal surrender that in the death to self, there is nothing of God to resist. When the self stops resisting God, then the marks of the crucified life will be evident upon the believer.

11.

SAMSON AND THE CRUCIFIED LIFE

The story of Samson is made popular particularly through his marriage to Delilah and his subsequent downfall. There is so much to gain in our understanding as believers about that man and the message of the crucified life. His story is set out for us in Judges 13–16 and his name appears only again in Hebrews 11.

S amson was born to fulfil a particular and specific purpose. It was to *begin* the final deliverance of Israel from the Philistines according to the prophetic word of the angel of the Lord (13:5). In this regard, Samson's spiritual purpose was clear. The story begins by explaining the state of the nation of Israel. It was a continued cycle of disobedience, the people falling into the hand of the enemies as an act of God's judgment, the people then calling out to God for deliverance, God sending them a deliverer, the people delivered and the cycle begins again with disobedience.

But this deliverer was to be different, he was to begin the breaking of this cycle in which the people of God found themselves. His purpose was clearly set out for him. It was defining, it was definite.

Sadly, the text begins with the people in the hands of the Philistines and ends with the deliver in the hands of the Philistines. How could this be? There are several observations to make in the life of Samson which might help us to appreciate what happened.

TAKING POSITIONAL BLESSINGS FOR GRANTED

Samson knew who he was. His name means 'light,' a clear indication of what God intended for him and what his parents hoped for him. He was a miracle child, the product of barren parents. He was special. He knew the prophetic word spoken over him and evidently took for granted that nothing could prevent the fulfilment of that word in his life. He was a Nazirite, chosen from birth. He knew that God's hand was upon him. He came to believe that it did not matter if he took care of his spiritual health, he would still be able to exercise the spiritual authority as he always did and God's will would be fulfilled in his life.

He was one of the very few OT saints who had this tremendous mark and manifestation of the power and the presence of the Holy Spirit upon his life.

1. The woman gave birth to a boy and named him Samson. He grew and the LORD blessed him, and the Spirit of the LORD began to stir him while he was in Mahaneh Dan, between Zorah and Eshtaol (1: 24- 25).

2. The Spirit of the LORD came upon him in power so that he tore the lion apart with his bare hands as he might have torn a young goat. But he told neither his father nor his mother what he had done (2:6).

3. Then the Spirit of the LORD came upon him in power. He went down to Ashkelon, struck down thirty of their men, stripped them of their belongings and gave their clothes to those who had explained the riddle (2:19).

4. As he approached Lehi, the Philistines came toward him shouting. The Spirit of the LORD came upon him in power. The ropes on his arms became like charred flax, and the bindings dropped from his hands. Finding a fresh jawbone of a donkey, he grabbed it and struck down a thousand men (15:14–15)

Interestingly, after his death, Samson was buried in the very place where the Holy Spirit first stirred him between Zorah and Eshtaol (13:25 cf. 16:31).

There can be no doubt that this Man was mightily used of God in the encounter with the Philistines, but what was also clear from the text is that Samson also used his gift for very selfish ends as well, quite apart from the direct and deliberate work of the Holy Spirit.

The catching of the three hundred foxes and torching of the orchards was purely out of a spirit of revenge. He lost a woman he should never have had in the first place and used his gift to demonstrate his rage. The girl and her father were burnt to death as a consequence of Samson's selfish use of his gift.

Samson also used his strength improperly to elude capture after he went to spend the night with a prostitute. Knowing that the place was surrounded, he inappropriately used the gifting that God gave him to tear off the gates and the pillars of the gates to make his escape.

But as well, Samson used his gift as sport. There was no sense of remorse for what he did. In the episode of killing the lion, it was the power of the Holy Spirit which empowered him so to do. But he violated his Nazarite vow when he ate honey from the carcass of the lion, then deliberately gave some of the honey from the dead carcass to his parents, then went further to make a riddle of the wrong he did! Here Samson added sin upon sin in ignorant arrogance.

For us as Christians, there are different ways in which we find ourselves in similar circumstances. We know that we are called, anointed and appointed. We see the power and the presence of the Holy Spirit in our lives as we seek to live out the Christian life, but there is no sense of order, no sense of cohesion, no purposeful building towards a desired end.

It was God's will to confront the Philistines, but Samson did not even seem to be aware of it and seemed to do everything to impede it. He took for granted his knowledge of who he was in God and believed it to be a kind of shield which would bring him to his ultimate purpose, no matter how he lived.

CHARACTER FLAWS

Samson had a bad attitude to his spiritual purpose, but he also had some deep spiritual character flaws.

Rashness and emotional blindness

According to our text, the first words out of Samson's mouth were—"I have seen a Philistine woman in Timnah; now get her for me as my wife (14:2)" followed by, "Get her for me. She's the right one for me."

While the text clearly says, it was God's plan to confront the Philistines, Samson would not follow God's script. He would not listen to the counsel of his parents. Samson constantly flirted with the enemy, with this Philistine woman from Timnah, with the prostitute from Gaza and with Delilah from the Valley of Sorek.

There seemed to have been a deep inner hunger in Samson. It manifests itself in his eating honey from the carcass of the lion and his cry to God for water. There seemed to be in Samson a deep longing that he was never able to control, an emotional and spiritual emptiness that he tried to cover over in rash and empty relationships. Even though he was this great man of God, there was something dogging his steps which pushed him into these destructive relationships which eventually led him to captivity.

Women seemed to have him confused about love. The Timnite woman said to him—"You hate me! You don't really love me. You've given my people a riddle, but you haven't told me the answer" (14:16). And Delilah said to him, "How can you say, 'I love you,' when you won't confide in me? This is the third time you have made a fool of me and haven't told me the secret of your great strength" (16:15).

The cycle of sin which dogged Israel became the cycle of sin which dogged the man that God had set to deliver them. It was tragic to see in this man of so much potential, so much of the move of God and yet so much against what God wanted of him and expected of him.

Rage and Anger

It seemed that from early out, Samson's life was marked and marred by anger. Now the Bible clearly teaches the legitimacy of anger, but there is a point at which anger becomes destructive and it seems that repeatedly Samson's anger went way beyond that which was acceptable.

Listen to him in his anger:

> *This time I have a right to get even with the Philistines; I will really harm them.* (15:3)
> *Since you've acted like this, I won't stop until I get my revenge on you.* (15:7)
> *I merely did to them what they did to me.* (15:11)

Samson spoke as though vengeance was in his hand. He saw himself as having a right to get even, he saw himself on a crusade, not for God, but for the personal loss he suffered and was very nonchalant about the destruction he caused—"I merely did to them what they did to me." (15:11)

Invincibility

Samson believed himself to be invincible. He tells the three thousand men of Israel to tie him up. They did and he broke the cords with ease. Physically he was strong, but spiritually he was weak. He placed more faith in his gift that the God who gave him the gift.

His sense of invincibility did not rest in God, but what he saw manifest in his life. At 16:20, believing in his invincibility, he got up to do what he did before and did not realise that the Lord had left him.

There is no greater tragedy for any servant of God than to have greater faith in his gift than in the God who gives the gift. Samson made one fundamental error in his life and it was upon this point. He believed that his gift was at his disposal to use as he wished, not realising that it belonged to the Lord. It was not the gift which made him powerful, it was the Lord and he did not know this.

THE CONSEQUENCES

So the hero ends up in slavery, his eyes dug out, he is grinding at the mill of the Philistines, his hair gone. And even more disastrously, the Philistines are celebrating a great victory. They were praising their god Dagan that, he, Dagon had handed Samson over to them.

There is no worse place for a servant of God to find himself than to have his eyes plucked out, grinding at the mill of the enemy and to hear the ridicule of the of the people as they throw contempt at him and praise their god that the mighty man of God has fallen.

And yet, it took this very episode to bring Samson to his ultimate purpose. Sometimes we take the wrong road to the fulfilment of our purpose and find that it leads us there anyways!

A Nazarite who found that he has become unclean must bring a sacrifice to God. Samson had none to bring. He was in chains. But he could do one thing. He could make a sacrifice of himself. His last words were—"Let me die with the Philistines!"

The crucified life requires that—dying. The fulfilment of Samson's purpose lies in his willingness to die. He did fulfil the angel's prophecy. He killed more in this one act of dying than in all his twenty years of leading.

Samson previously held in his hands the dead jawbone of an ass. With it he slew a thousand men. It was a lesson that he was to learn. It was only as he surrendered himself to death that God would use him to slay three thousand men.

The crucified life is the beginning of a purposeful life. Samson would not know God's purpose and would not appear in the Hall of Faith without becoming in his death the man of faith.

There is much debate about whether Samson was saved. It's hard to look at a life with so many contradictions and believe that he was. And yet, there are several indicators in the text. While in prison the text reveals—But the hair on his head began to grow again after it had been shaved.

God always restores Hs people. What may be odious to us, what may be unforgivable to us, God treats with gentleness and kindness, mercy and grace where there is the willingness to be crucified.

And what more shall I say? I do not have time to tell about... Samson,... through faith conquered kingdoms... and gained what was promised... (Heb. 11: 32–33)

12.
MARKS OF THE CRUCIFIED LIFE

Therefore, since Christ suffered in his body, arm your-
selves with the same attitude, because he who has
suffered in his body is done with sin (1 Pet. 4: 1).

The person who comes to faith in the Lord Jesus Christ understands that he has been called to a life which involves
pain. Every serious believer understands this. There is a very
popular notion in Christian thinking which stresses God's promises of blessings in this life over the fact of pain and suffering.

In fact the miracles highlighted are very often the ones in
which there is some cure of some disease, deliverances from
some crises or the salvation of many souls. The fact is, there is
the miracle of God's grace in the midst of suffering, where the
sufferer is not relieved of his pain, but is given the grace of
God as the sufficient antidote to take one in pain and through
pain. That is a very special miracle which sometimes tells as
much of God's sovereign goodness, love and care as do the
more spectacular miracles of healing and deliverance from
crises and sicknesses.

Embracing the names of God which depict His grace and
role as deliver and saviour are important. These include:

- Jehovah Jireh—The Lord who provides. He is always
  there looking out for our needs, our physical needs in
  particular.
- Jehovah Shammah—The Lord who is always present.
  We need not worry because he is always there.
- Jehovah Rapha—the Lord who heals. This is a particularly popular one in a world crawling with so much disease and disorder

- Jehovah Shalom—the Lord our peace. Here again is the reminder of God acting on our behalf in the face of distress.
- Jehovah Nissi—the Lord our banner. This reminds us of God under whose victorious insignia we fight.
- Jehovah Rohi—the Lord our Shepherd. This speaks to the one who guides us and takes care of us
- Jehovah Tsidkenu—the Lord our righteousness, a reminder that our justification is in Him

All of these are precious to believers all over and rightly so. For God has promised that He would be and do these things on behalf of His people. But surely, these truths must not ignore the fact that God describes Himself in other ways as well.

JEHOVAH M'KADDESH—THE LORD WHO SANCTIFIES (LEV. 20:8)

Anyone who becomes devoted to the Lord must be first be put upon the altar of sacrifice. In a sense, it is the symbol of dying to the self and all its desires. Leviticus 27:26-29 makes the point very well. Verse 29 in particular is very clear—No person devoted to destruction may be ransomed; he must be put to death.

Persons who were dedicated to destruction could not be redeemed by anyone, nor could anyone keep them for any reason for themselves. This was where Saul, for instance, got into trouble with the prophet, as mentioned earlier.

Instead of destroying the Amelekites, recognising them as dedicated to the Lord, and in obedience to the Word of the Lord that as devoted things they were to be utterly destroyed, Saul decided to save what he wanted. He lost the Kingdom because he violated "the principle of the devoted thing."

The same is also true of Achan. He kept back was dedicated to the Lord under the floor of his tent. He and his house died as a result of doing this. As with most spiritual principle, there is always a multiplied in effect in the actions of those whose ideas and actions defy the will of the Lord. That which becomes dedicated to the Lord, requires destruction, or if it cannot be destroyed, it is left in a secure place, where no man's hands may touch it, save the Lord's who decides what He wants to become acceptable to Him.

The thing dedicated to the Lord bears His stamp of ownership. His holiness comes upon it and any who touch it apart from those designated to will certainly face His hot displeasure. This is why Uzzah also got into trouble. The Ark of the Covenant was not his to carry or even to touch. When the oxen stumbled, he reached out to steady the ark, to save it from falling, but he died. He was not to touch it.

Every believer knows that sanctification costs and God describes Himself in this way to remind us that He is the one who does in our lives what needs to be done so that we might be presented before His throne as holy, and without spot or wrinkle.

In sanctification, the believer understands that his desire and his pleasure take second place to what God intends that He should have and be. It cannot be overstated that God wants to build in us through sanctification, the character of His Son. If the process is painful, then so be it; the objective is our completion in Christlikeness, not our comfort in the self life.

THE GOD WHO STRIKES
(ISAIAH 9:13; EZEKIEL 7:9)

The Hebrew expression here is a derivative of the one quoted above. It seems here however that God will act is ways that His servants might find unpleasant. The striking of the Lord is to bring discipline and order to the family of God and God will not restrain Himself from acting in this fashion.

Remember how He treated Miriam when she incited Aaron and together they rose up against Moses. In Numbers 12:10ff. God was very clear about the situation. Having struck Miriam with leprosy, the Lord described it as if her father had spat in her face.

The striking of the Lord cannot be a pleasant experience, but it is a necessary and an important part of our formation into what He wants of us.

OUR FATHER... OUR POTTER
(ISAIAH 64:8)

This text reminds us that we are indeed like pottery in the hand of God. He decides what shape we will take and what purpose will be made of us. Isaiah 29: 16 has a most interesting rendering. There it says—You turn things upside down, as if the potter were the clay!

In shaping us, things may seem confusing. Things may seem difficult to understand on the human level, but God is very clear about what He is doing and what He intends to accomplish.

In fact, sometimes things even seem to be working in reverse when the Potter is at work. There are some very interesting oxymora in the scriptures, but none is as popular and as potent as Jesus' maxim- to live you must first die.

What we may observe from the above then is that quite apart from the fact that God intervenes in our lives for our temporal help and benefit there are times when His intervention is to mould us towards His purpose and His will. This might be very difficult and the crucified life requires the kind of attitude which acknowledges God's sovereign right to exact in us whatever pleases Him.

There are those whose faith only take them to the point of believing God and trusting Him only when the times are good. Jesus describes them in the Parable of the sower in Matthew 13. Such, He says, are those who receive the word but have no root and so when the troubles and the persecutions come because of the Word they fall away. Or they are like those who hear the word, but the worries of life and the seduction of wealth make them unfruitful.

So, trouble will come. This is the aspect of the Christian life which is the mark of the crucifying of the self. It is seeing Jesus with the blood dripping from His side, from his hands, from his feet and running down in His face.

It is not about being morbid, but rather recognising that without death of self as embodied in the soul's response to the world, the sinful nature, to legalism and to principalities and powers, then living the victorious Christian life that the believer seeks becomes impossible.

As a consequence there must be the recognition of the importance of being yielded to the cross from which there must be no squirming.

VULNERABLE

In the crucified life there must be vulnerability. Being vulnerable means that the believer becomes open and exposed to whatever God wills for him. But vulnerability is not an external given. It first has to be cultivated on the inside. David, after his coveting his neighbours wife, his adultery, his murder of Uriah, and his deceptive and arrogance behaviour comes to his sense and admits in Psalm 51 that what God desires is truth in the inward parts.

Probably the defining mark of the crucified life is the mark of vulnerability. In vulnerability there is willing exposure and surrender to the glare of God. David prayed that God would search him. I suppose that even in this elemental stage of human development, this king understood the danger of self examination if the conscience and the will are weakened and threatened.

Vulnerability allows the believer to place his trust completely in God, without fear of what God might or might not do. In modern times, vulnerability has come to mean weakness, but it is not so among those who are crucified. It is the essence of being yielded to God, the only basis upon which spiritual obedience will have any meaning.

The main reason why believers find themselves in all kinds of spiritual trouble, pain and heartache is in the fact that vulnerability is being sacrificed to protect pride and to prevent exposure.

Some believers feel no need to be open to anyone. They hide their hurts, they hide their pain, they hide their sorrows, and they hide their joys. They have no friends upon whom they can truly call. For some of these believers, they will have more persons to carry their coffins at their funerals than persons with whom they could honestly share their real selves while they were alive.

Think of it for a moment—the persons taking you to your final resting place never knew you, but are probably performing this task out of duty, out of respect or out of association.

This secrecy has done much to damage believers and malign the body of Christ. The rejection of spiritual vulnerability to God and to fellow believers for the embrace of self- protection and self-preservation invariably backfires. Everyone is damaged by it and the thing we hoped that we would have been preserved from becomes the source of our public shame.

Any individual believer who lives his life without going the way of the cross, not now in the salvific sense that he might be saved, but in the sense of making himself vulnerable to the will and purpose of God, that Christ might be manifest in him, has not yet begun to understand what it means to live for Jesus. Paul tells Timothy of those who are learning but never coming to knowledge of the truth. Invariably, their heads and minds are full of knowledge, but their spirits remain untouched.

To live without vulnerability to Christ is to live a second rated Christian life, and yet, how can one be called a believer, a Christian, if he does not make himself truly vulnerable to the One who was made vulnerable for him? And yet it seems true that there are believers who are truly saved, but whose salvation experience limit them only to the knowledge of salvation, that they have been freely justified in Christ, but who never go towards growing in death, death to self.

BROKEN

Vulnerability leads to brokenness before God. Brokenness is a condition of the heart and the will where the heart in the act of surrender to the will of God is broken and the self life flows out so that the heart may be re-energised by the power of God. To become broken requires an acknowledgement of the desperate incapacity to achieve anything apart from God. Brokenness is that capacity, if it may be called a capacity to surrendered oneself because of known incapacity, so that that which is out of order can be fixed by God.

When we become vulnerable too, the brokenness we encounter might not be God's doing but it may well be the effect of the wounds inflicted upon us because we have become vulnerable. This is a distinct possibility. Every crucified individual must suffer brokenness.

David laments that it is the person who goes up with him who lifts the heel against him. And believers all over have known the trauma and the horror of being wounded by those who have been accusing and abusive, even those within the community of believers.

STILLNESS

In the midst of brokenness too, the crucified life is marked by stillness. There is something obvious about something which is dead—it cannot move by itself. Stillness then requires a dependence upon another source for vitality and existence. The crucified life demands stillness, so that the surgical tools of God might be applied with undue interference.

But stillness must also mean the willingness to turn the other cheek, as Jesus put it. Turning the other cheek is not cowardice, for He could have called angels to His defence. Turning the other cheek is that confident knowledge in the midst of pain that vindication is not to be found in the self, but is in the Lord.

Self promotion never helps. It is those who wait patiently in the context of the pain of crucifixion who eventually mount up with wings as eagles. Those who trust in themselves, like strong young men trusting in their strength will eventually get weary. But those who trust patiently in God will see Him raising them up as it pleases Him.

13.
THE LORD'S TABLE

For whenever you eat this bread and drink this cup you proclaim the Lord's death until he comes (1 Cor. 11:26)

A BACKWARD LOOK

A careful reading of the Lord's Table shows how time collapses in this one sacred event. It is first of all a memorial. Jesus commands the believer to break the bread and drink the cup in memory of Him, who He is and what He did at Calvary.

The memorial is an awesome and graphic picture of the reality of the life and the death of Jesus. While much is to be made of the resurrection of Jesus, and without it, our faith would be meaningless, Paul makes the point that in the Table, we proclaim, or we preach the crucifixion and the death of Jesus.

Every time we break a piece of the bread from the loaf, we know that it represents our taking from that Body and to ourselves all that Jesus intended His crucifixion to mean for us. And every time we drink from that cup, we know that we are drinking from a cup of suffering, death and new life—spiritual life.

There is a sense in which the emblems bring death and life to the same Table. In the same way they symbolise death, they also symbolise life. But the Table is first of all the proclamation, not of life, but of surrender, suffering and death.

When the believer begins to understand this, then his perspective begins to change, for there is "death in the cup." It is the death of self, death to the world, death to sin, death to the law and death to principalities and powers. In the bread and the cup, the believer commemorates crucifixion and the empowerment that Jesus gives him which makes it possible for him to truly die.

In coming to the Table then, we acknowledge that Jesus' work is done and in Him, our status is sealed. When He died, we died with Him and our old self has been left there at the cross.

A PRESENT REALITY

But the Table is not only a backward look. It is a present examination. Paul commands that as we take the bread and drink the cup, we must examine ourselves.

The present reality requires examination, because there must be in our present reality the truth of the facts of the events we commemorate. There is a world of difference between what is true and what is fact. The fact is that in Jesus, we died to sin, but is that fact true in the believer's present reality?

Coming to the Table is coming to a place of examination to discover the truth concerning how much we have appropriated the proclamation. In taking the bread and the cup, we preach the death of Jesus. But in taking the emblems, we preach ourselves too, as dead to the very things that the scriptures declare us free from.

The taking of the bread and the cup seals to the world our greatest declaration of what is true about us, for in sharing in the emblems, we declare to the world, the flesh and principalities and powers that we are free from their grasp and control and that we have active dominion over them.

The Table is the place of an acknowledgement of personal vulnerability to God and to others. It is the place of brokenness that we might find wholeness and it is the place of stillness that God may breathe in us again the power and the will to live the way He wants us to live.

A FUTURE ANTICIPATION

Every child of God has this burning in his heart—the desire to see Jesus again. When the believer comes to take the cup, he takes it knowing that it is a temporary arrangement. It is to be taken *until* Jesus comes. There is so much locked up in this one thought.

The taking of the cup has in view the ultimate redemption— the fulfilment of the promise, the honouring of the "Promissory Note" deposited in us.

The significance must not be missed because it is only until then that sorrow and mourning and tears and pain shall be removed. Death, the final enemy, will be thrown into the Lake of Fire and will cease to be a reality among the people of God.

The proclamation of the death of Jesus and our death in Him on this side of eternity, will give way to a new proclamation, a proclamation which affirms life, the absolute and unconditional lifting of the curse of sin and the celebration of the wedding feast of the Lamb.

In this one event, time coalesces—the past, the present and the future unite and the believer is transported across the limitations of time, to being taken to the very Throne Room of God in that one solitary act of worship.

Jesus set the crucified life as the paradigm which identifies the covenant people. Without the crucified life, there is nothing to proclaim. Paul insists on it. He argues in several places for this point. He wanted to know nothing except Christ crucified. To some it's a stumbling block; to others it is simply offensive.

The tragedy for some in the faith is that the Table has become a place of sentimentalism and for others the re-enforcement of tribal traditionalism. But the power of the Table lies in the fact that the believer comes to remember Christ crucified—the crucified life. It is this which defines the faith—the hardship and suffering, of blood oozing, of flesh torn. Even in heaven, while every injury the believer ever bore will be totally repaired, Jesus will still bear the marks of the injuries He suffered on our behalf. He is the Lamb slain before the foundations of the earth were laid. And the Table takes us across time, to celebrate a God who in eternity past carried in Himself our wounds, who when He lived, was taken to the old rugged cross, and now that He is exalted, still carries in His hands, His side, His feet and His face, the insignia of One having been slain. The only marks of injury in heaven will be those carried by Jesus.

THE SYMBOL OF THE NEW COVENANT

The Table spread before the believer is the sign of the New Covenant. Under the Old Covenant, the gathering for fellowship and memorial was concerning a day—Remember the Sabbath Day. In the New Covenant the gathering for fellowship and memorial is around a Person and instead of remembering the Old World and the creation of that world, the believer now declares the death of Jesus, the seed planted to bring life and immortality to a new world and a new order—the world of the spirit, for flesh and blood cannot inherit the kingdom of God.

When Jesus first raised the question of His followers eating His flesh and drinking His blood, many turned away from Him. They did not understand it. In their minds it was a revolting thought. But the uniting of Himself with the believer was what Jesus had in mind

It was the painful giving of Himself that others might learn from Him and find life, hope, purpose and meaning in a new creation as new creatures, empowered to live under the rule of the King of kings and Lord of lords.

A lot is true in what we affirm. In the cross we recall that Jesus died for us. We proclaim His death until He comes. But we must not forget this key truth which is fundamental to our faith—the Table reminds us that we share in His suffering. It reminds us that just as He suffered we too are called to suffer.

I think that this is the missing dimension in the observing of the Lord's Table. When the believer goes to the Table, he must remind himself that the death of Jesus is also the place where he too dies. It does not shift the focus from Christ but it magnifies it. If more time were spent in those quiet moments meditating on the events of the cross as personal, then the quality of the sanctified life would be much different.

While this might not be a significant thought, it seems to me that those who celebrate the Lord's Supper with great frequency ought to be the ones who have a better appreciation of what it means to live the crucified life. When they take the bread in their hands every Sunday, they say to the world, I am crucified with Christ.

When they take the cup, they are acknowledging that the blood of Jesus is their only source of life. Every week they faithfully do this, but without recognising that the Table, that it is not just a symbol, but the embodiment of the reality of personal daily crucifixion, then they would have missed it. For what Christ accomplished once for all and then sat down, we must appropriate daily and having done all to stand.

The Lord's Table then must serve to shift our gaze to include the proclamation that in the death of Christ the individual believer is crucified. And not only is he crucified but the world is dead to him, the law is dead to him, the sinful nature is dead to him and principalities and powers are dead to him.

The believer who takes the cup and breaks the bread without recognising that the death of Jesus, that in His death Jesus became vulnerable, broken and still, and therefore in that death he is represented, that believer disowns the very Person of whom the symbol speaks.

Paul talks of it and it should bring fear to the heart of every saint. It seems then that when the believer comes to the Table and does not recognise that in the death of Jesus he too dies and he walks away from the Table to live a life which does not know crucifixion, he has just taken judgment upon himself.

What a tragedy it would be if the believer repeats this Sunday after Sunday and not recognise the body of the Lord. It would be an awful tragedy indeed if he touches the sacred symbol memorialising the New Covenant.

PART III:
THE CRUCIFIED LIVE
DEVOTIONAL

THE CRUCIFIED LIFE:
A 40-DAY JOURNEY

INTRODUCTION

This devotional guide will help in the assimilation of the information shared herein. The intention is to help to make the work relevant, applicable and relatable in our day-to-day living out of the Crucified Life.

Used with the main work, it can be useful for personal study, family devotions, or group workshops. It can also be used by churches and other ministries as material to systematically take the group through learning about this aspect of Christian life and practice. It can be used for Bible Study sessions by the whole church or by small groups within the church.

This resource can also be used by Bible Schools and Seminaries as an important tool to develop thought and discipline and to broaden the scope of information and interaction on this very important area of the spiritual journey, particularly in courses having to do with spiritual formation.

This forty- day journey focussed on the crucified life covers the material in the book and can be used by the individual, group or wider congregation as a systematic study of this theme. In that sense, it may be used over specific period, such as during the Lenten season. Additionally, an individual or church may undertake this particular study in a sustained way over a given particular period of time. This study-guide is also a useful online tool which can be used individually or collectively for online studies or discussions. The ultimate goal of course is that the people of God may be strengthened by it, to impact a world in need of transformative people on a mission for kingdom building.

DAY ONE:
WHAT HAPPENED THAT DAY

...they crucified Him (Mark 15:24-25)

Book Reading: Chapter One—From the Garden to the Tomb
Scripture Focus: Wrestling in Prayer (Matt. 26:36-46; Mark 14:32-42, Luke 22:39-46)

The days leading up to the death of Jesus and Crucifixion Day itself are the most significant days in human history. Having instituted the sign of the New Covenant, commonly called the Lord's Table, Jesus began His trek to Gethsemane which ultimately would lead to the Cross. It was this New Covenant which was to create a new humanity and offer hope to everyone who would put his or her faith in Jesus. Being in the Garden was a time of intense wrestling in prayer. It was so intense that His sweat became great drops of blood, as it were.

Our thought for reflection here is that prayer is no ordinary weapon in living The Crucified Life. Jesus prayed about the fulfilment of His purpose and demonstrated through His prayer that there was no other way to fulfil this purpose, but by the way of taking the cup.

What is the place of prayer in our pursuit of living the Crucified Life? Do you think your Prayer Life might need some attention?

Prayer at its holiest moment is the entering into God [where] miracles seem tame... by comparison. —A.W. Tozer

DAY TWO:
WHAT HAPPENED THAT DAY

...they crucified Him (Mark 15:24-25)

Book Reading: Chapter One—From the Garden to the Tomb
Scripture Focus: Arrested (Mark 14:43-52; Luke 22:47-53; John 18:1-11)

There is something humiliating about being arrested. God— arrested by His creatures. Jesus now allows Himself to be arrested in the interest of the very imprisoned humanity He came to set free.

The Crucified Life in this regard is the display of meekness in the face of the place of humiliation. It is the display of self-control when it seems that the worst kind of injustice was about to be meted out to the King of Glory.

Peter wanted to help, to correct the narrative in righteous indignation, but the hour did not require that. There was no place for Peter's well intended attempt at dealing with the in-justice of the moment. Others fled, to save themselves.

The Crucified Life is the surrender of the soul in the face of the maddening crowd that, that very crowd may one by one come to its senses. It was the Centurion and those with him who at the cross agreed, "Indeed, this was truly the Son of God!" Matt. 27: 54

How do we feel in the face of the discomfort and threats that come at us when we are seeking to fulfil God's will? What do you do when your closest friends want to take matters in their own hands on your behalf, or when they run away, when it is obvious that you are not acting to save yourself?

The person who bears and suffers evils with meekness and silence is the sum of a Christian man. —Charles Wesley

DAY THREE:
WHAT HAPPENED THAT DAY

...they crucified Him (Mark 15:24-25)

Book Reading*: Chapter One—From the Garden to the Tomb
Scripture Focus: Jesus before Jewish Officialdom (Matt. 26:57–68; Mk. 14:53–65; Luke 22:66–71; John 18:12–24)

Officialdom has a way of seeking to publicly or secretly force conformity. The Crucified Life refuses to be forced into any conformity outside of what God requires. Indeed, it will soon be found that in its attempt to force conformity and compliance, officialdom will soon break its own rules. The High Priest ends up tearing his robe which the law forbad (Lev. 21:10)

Annas and Caiaphas were leading men who were committed to protecting and safeguarding the status quo, especially since it served their own interests. There was a deeper interest to be served, however. It was the will and the plan of God. These religious and pious men missed it.

It is this willingness to be spiritually defiant in humility which marks the Crucified Life. Jesus would not budge. It says, in effect, that there was nothing to hide, nothing to recoil from, and nothing to change His mind about.

How willing are we to face the power structures around us to simply be true to who God has called us to be and to do what He has set out for us to do?

Contrary to what might be expected, I look back on experiences that at the time seemed especially desolating and painful, with particular satisfaction. Indeed, I can say with complete truthfulness that everything I have learned in my seventy-five years in this world, everything that has truly enhanced and enlightened my existence, has been through affliction and not through happiness, whether pursued or attained... This, of course, is what the Cross signifies. And it is the Cross, more than anything else, that has called me inexorably to Christ. —Malcolm Muggeridge

DAY FOUR: WHAT HAPPENED THAT DAY

...they crucified Him (Mark 15:24-25)

Book Reading: Read Chapter One—From the Garden to the Tomb

Scripture Focus: Jesus Before the Romans (John 18:28-19:16; Luke 23: 1-25; Mark 15:1-20; Matt.27: 11-26)

Rejection pierces as nothing else does. John reminds us that Jesus came to His own, but His own did not receive Him. The sting of rejection is not easily overcome, especially if you know that your own character, your work and your intention all warrant a good reception.

And worst, it seemed that the only whisper of some frail hope of acceptance was coming from a tenuous foreigner—Pilate, who at the last minute, on account of political pressure and expedience gave in to the maddening crowd. Indeed, there was no basis to kill Jesus, except that He said He was the King of the Jews.

There will always be those who balk at the truth you represent, and when you have given your best, they still treat you with suspicion and some outright choose others over you. The Crucified Life recognises that in self-surrender you will be rejected by others.

How do we treat those who have been eager to see the end of us, those who want to make you feel like you don't belong, like you don't fit? What attitude have you displayed to the ringleader of the group plotting your destruction?

There can be no deep disappointment where there is not deep love. —Martin Luther King, Jr.

DAY FIVE:
THE SURRENDERED LIFE

Come down from the cross and save yourself! (Mark 15:30)

Book Reading: Read Chapter Two—The Surrendered Life

The sight of Jesus hanging there on the cross was not the beautiful sentimental syrupy stuff of Hollywood blockbusters. He was telling of His burning thirst, offering forgiveness to a repentant criminal, another offer of forgiveness to the maddening crowd, offering the care of His mom to one of His disciples, torn at the fact that His Father had forsaken Him, committing His Spirit into the hands of His Father as He died, and that that cry—"It is finished!"

His nakedness was for all to see. Blood "rivered" from His head, His hands, His feet, His back and His face. Because of the crown of thorns that was beaten into His skull, even the blowing of a gentle breeze against His face was torture.

His emotions were raw. They laughed in His face, spat at Him and mocked His power. They cynically ridiculed him, challenging Him to save Himself, probably slapping each other's backs as they did.

When we see the Cross, what do we see?

Come, and see the victories of the cross. Christ's wounds are thy healings, His agonies thy repose, His conflicts thy conquests, His groans thy songs, His pains thine ease, His shame thy glory, His death thy life, His sufferings thy salvation. —Matthew Henry

DAY SIX:
THE SURRENDERED LIFE

Come down from the cross and save yourself! (Mark 15:30)

Book Reading: Read Chapter Two—Death By the Cross
Scripture Focus: Death by the Cross (Isaiah 53:10, Acts 2:23)

There was no worst kind of death than death by the cross. The Romans did not allow their citizens to experience capital punishment in that manner. It was too degrading, to humiliating, too dehumanising. Philippians 2 explains the level to which Jesus was willing to go. It was no half-way surrender. It was not a three-quarter way surrender. The Crucified Life requires full surrender to the will of God.

Jesus did not end His ministry by dying peacefully in His sleep one night in Jerusalem. What He needed to do in fulfilling the will of God required the cross, the full ordeal of the cross. He experienced death in every way as He hung here – physical death, emotional death and spiritual death. The wages of sin is death.

The Crucified Life requires a similar embrace of death. It is only as we respond fully to the will of God that we discover that there are things— attitudes, character and personality traits, personal hopes and dreams that must be fully and properly surrendered that God's will may come to pass in us. What is our response to the direction that God has been calling us in respect to us and His purpose? Are we trying to save ourselves from death?

To know the Cross is not merely to know our own sufferings. For the Cross is the sign of salvation, and no man is saved by his own sufferings. To know the Cross is to know that we are saved by the sufferings of Christ; more,

it is to know the love of Christ who underwent suffering and death in order to save us. It is, then, to know Christ.
—Thomas Merton

DAY SEVEN:
THE SURRENDERED LIFE

Come down from the cross and save yourself! (Mark 15:30)

Book Reading : Read Chapter Two—Leaving Ourselves at the Cross
Scripture Focus: Leaving ourselves at the cross (John 19:38, Mark 15:34)

One of the best tests of our character lies in how we re-spond in our pain particularly to those who hurt us. And it is those who hurt us first and most that we must first and most embrace in the Crucified Life. There is no place in the Crucified Life to love only those who love us, or to say "hello" only to those who tell us "hello" or to greet only those at song service that belong to the clique of us.

The thirst for God in the Crucified Life supersedes my own thirst for self-satisfaction. It demands that I forgive those who have not even asked for forgiveness, it demands that I offer hope to the person hanging on the cross beside me, even though my pain might be greater than his. It demands that even though we may cry at God and ask Him hard questions, that we never lose focus.

How have I been dealing with my pain in the face of the pain that others are feeling? How are you dealing with the pain of those who have hurt you and who have offended you, some-times when it feels that God has forsaken you?

It's so much easier to pray for a bore than to go and see one. —C.S. Lewis

Day Eight:
The Surrendered Life

Come down from the cross and save yourself! (Mark 15:30)

Book Reading: Read Chapter Two—The Cross as Symbol of Surrender

Scripture Focus: The Symbol of Surrender (John 12:25, 1 Cor. 2:14, Proverbs 3:5-6)

In living The Crucified Life our best faculties very often get in the way. Our sense of reason will give us a million explanations why this cannot work, or why this is the thing to do. Our emotions will seduce us into taking another path, usually an easier path or a path of selfishness.

This is why the Crucified Life does not only see us giving up our bad ways but it sees us giving up our good ways as well. Someone once remarked that even our tears of repentance must be washed in the blood of the lamb. The cross is above all else the symbol of surrender to find true life, but it also smells of death.

What is it that needs to be put to death that stands in the way of that Crucified Life that we seek? Often these are not bad things—such as our personalities, or things we simply prefer. We must always remember that spiritual things are first spiritually discerned.

God grant me the serenity to accept the things I cannot change, courage to change the things I can, and the wisdom to know the difference. —Reinhold Niebuhr

Day Nine:
The Surrendered Life

Come down from the cross and save yourself! (Mark 15:30)

Book Reading: Read Chapter Two—Learning Obedience through Crucifixion
Scripture Focus: Take Everything (Job 1: 9-12)

Sometimes, it seems that God's promises are suspended between the earth and heaven. You really can't tell what heaven is up to. As you try to work your way through, you have a sense that God is either not hearing, too busy or it seems that everyone else is getting through, while you are somehow left on the back burner.

There is that risk of feeling sorry for ourselves. But the Crucified Life is no place to feel sorry for ourselves, even when it seems that God is stripping us. That kind of disposition betrays a loss of faith in who God is, His character, His promises and His purpose. It is not always easy, but it is required and the waiting helps to shape us in the Crucified Life.

What is happening in our space regarding the seeming delays of God? What is happening when it seems that God is taking everything from you? Are you still trusting? Are you getting frustrated? Are you getting disappointed with God?

Self-pity is easily the most destructive of the non-pharmaceutical narcotics; it is addictive, gives momentary pleasure and separates the victim from reality. —John Gardner

DAY TEN:
THE SURRENDERED LIFE

"Come down from the cross and save yourself!" (Mark 15:30)

Book Reading: Read Chapter Two—Crucified to Find Life
Scripture Focus: Willing and Acting (Phil. 2:13 Gal. 2:19-20).

We may not truly live until we are truly dead! This is one of the important paradoxes of the scriptures, and the sooner we discover and understand it the better our journey will be. Indeed it is central to the Crucified Life.

As we allow the Holy Spirit to put us to death, we soon discover that the way to life has been through Him all along. God does not merely want us to live right. He wants to live out His life in us. It is the outflow of that Christ-life which demonstrates that we are crucified.

What do we consider to be the main things preventing us from experiencing the flow of the Holy Spirit in our lives? What do you think is preventing the Holy Spirit from manifesting in you as you would love to experience?

We take what we think are the tools of spiritual transformation into our own hands and try to sculpt ourselves into robust Christlike specimens. But spiritual transformation is primarily the work of the Holy Spirit. He is the Master Sculptor. —Jerry Bridges

DAY ELEVEN: THE SURRENDERED LIFE

"Come down from the cross and save yourself!" (Mark 15:30)

Book Reading: Read Chapter Two—The Fallen Seed
Scripture Focus: The Fallen Seed (John 12: 20-34)

When a seed begins its fall to the ground, it is no longer in the "hand" of the farmer, but it still remains in the motive of the farmer. The safety of the hands of the farmer is surrendered to this new space. The seed is in free fall until it hits the ground, and there another process begins which "kills" that seed so that, that which is in that seed might begin to manifest, a manifestation which is not possible unless the seed falls and "dies."

The essence of The Crucified Life is that willingness to allow the process of dying. It is fear and pride which often get in the way and which resist this process, this process of becoming more like Jesus. The falling of the seed is critical if that process is to take place successfully. It is being willing to let go of the known, the predictable and the safe.

Sometimes we become content. Pride has that effect on us. The contentment with the sameness and the predictability of our spiritual space will prevent us from dying, from being fallen down in surrender.

How have we been trying to save ourselves from falling and dying? How have you tried to navigate around the only way to truly be like Jesus?

Pride must die in you, or nothing of heaven can live in you. —Andrew Murray

DAY TWELVE:
THE POWER OF SUFFERING

For it has been granted to you on behalf of Christ not only to believe on Him, but also to suffer for him... (Phil. 1:30)

Book Reading: Read Chapter Three—the Power of Suffering
Scripture Focus: Suffering for Him (Rom. 8:17, 2 Tim. 3:12, 1 Peter 4:16, Acts 14:21-22)

...participating in his sufferings, becoming like him in his death (Phil. 3:10)

These words from Paul have echoed down through the ages. Every child of God must hear them and prepare his or her heart to take on the full-frontal force of what they mean.

Paul was willing and prepared to become like Him in the ugliness of this suffering. It was no easy, light, superficial scarring. For him, the Crucified Life was not a way for an easy life in the here and now and certainly was not one of popularity, pleasantry and premium positions.

The truth though is that we can come to believe that we deserve better, and we deserve more at the hands of our God. We are often tempted to shy away from the suffering that the Crucified Life brings. Who can truly endure blood running down into his face, into his eyes without being able to wipe it away? Who truly can bear that kind of suffering?

Character cannot be developed in ease and quiet. Only through experience of trial and suffering can the soul be strengthened, ambition inspired, and success achieved.
—Helen Keller

DAY THIRTEEN:
THE POWER OF SUFFERING

For it has been granted to you on behalf of Christ not only to believe on Him, but also to suffer for him... (Phil. 1: 30)

Book Reading: Read Chapter Three—The Prosperity Doctrine and Suffering
Scripture Focus: Broken Vessel (2 Cor. 1:8, 2 Cor. 6:3-10).

Fredrick Pryce, Pastor of Word of Faith in Los Angeles is re-puted as saying,

...how can you glorify God in your body, when it doesn't function right? How can you glorify God? How can He get glory when your body doesn't even work?... What makes you think the Holy Ghost wants to live inside a body where He can't see out through the windows, and He can't hear with the ears? What makes you think the Holy Spirit wants to live inside of a physical body where the limbs and the organs and the cells do not function right?... And what makes you think He wants to live in a temple where He can't see out of the eyes, and He can't walk with the feet, and He can't move with the hand?... The only eyes that he has that are in the earth realm are the eyes that are in the body. If He can't see out of them then God's gonna be limited he's not going to be helped...

How seriously are we to take preachers like this in the face of great men and women who served without limbs, without sight, held together by nuts and bolts from a surgery after a tragic accident, but who love the Lord intensely. What do I tell my dear friend Rolda James?

He has chosen not to heal me, but to hold me. The more intense the pain, the closer His embrace. —Joni Eareckson Tada

DAY FOURTEEN: THE POWER OF SUFFERING

For it has been granted to you on behalf of Christ not only to believe on Him, but also to suffer for him... (Phil. 1:30)

Book Reading: Read Chapter Three—the Source of Suffering
Scripture Focus: The Marks of Christ. (Gal. 6:17, John 16:33).

Paul says, "Let no one cause me trouble, for I bear in my body the marks of Jesus." Faith in Jesus means trouble before the world. It means an angry and hostile world is going to respond. The world has no love for the people of faith and it will pour out its anger on every person of faith.

The enemy is equally hostile to every person of faith and will create every scheme to devour those who seek to walk by faith. The word teaches that that which is not based on faith is sin (Rom. 14:23), and consequently, the faith walk is challenged by the enemy at every turn.

The sin nature seeks to pull us in as we seek to honour this life of faith. This ongoing war and these enemies are strong, forceful and unapologetic. When they can't get us, they go after those we love and care deeply about to get us to genuflect.

Which of these enemies is coming after you strongest in their attempt to get you to let go? Tell of some of your personal faith scars.

The scars you share become lighthouses for other people who are headed to the same rocks you hit. —Jon Acuff

DAY FIFTEEN:
THE POWER OF SUFFERING

For it has been granted to you on behalf of Christ not only to believe on Him, but also to suffer for him... (Phil. 1:30)

Book Reading: Read Chapter Three—Jesus had to suffer
Scripture Focus: He had to suffer (Acts 17:3)

There is an inevitability to suffering. It's a kind of rite of passage, and indeed an important part of the passage itself for all who would walk with God. Scriptures remind us that it was God's will to strike Jesus.

Now this does not mean that the Father simply started to beat up on His Son. But it certainly means that the way of the cross was an agreement that was inescapable for both Father and Son. If the cross was agreed to then the implications of the cross were also agreed to. Living The Crucified Life therefore means agreeing to the consequences of the cross. So in the same way the Son had to suffer, in a similar way, the believer has to suffer.

Carrying the cross means pain for every child of God. It is the same for you too. How have you been managing your journey with your cross?

I have never thought that a Christian would be free of suffering... For our Lord suffered. And I came to believe that he suffered, not to save us from suffering, but to teach us how to bear suffering. For he knew that there is no life without suffering. —Alan Paton

DAY SIXTEEN:
THE POWER OF SUFFERING

For it has been granted to you on behalf of Christ not only to believe on Him, but also to suffer for him... (Phil. 1:30)

Book Reading: Read Chapter Three—Suffering Brings Dependence upon God

Scripture Focus: Suffering Brings Dependence upon God (2 Cor. 1:3–11)

In Paul's own experience he talks of suffering as being weakened so that he might find his strength in God. This is not normal to the selfish ear, or the arrogant ear. We want our own, to build our own, to be dependent on no one and to ensure that no one can make any claims on us.

There is no such place as self-reliance in the Crucified Life. It knows no notion that God helps those who help themselves. At its most sacred level, the Crucified Life is the recognition of our need to be completely dependent on God through the blessed Holy Spirit. Without that dependence, we will never be able to live the way that God wants us to live. We must not then empty ourselves of the things that make us weak, but importantly, we must empty ourselves of the things that make us self-reliant, so that we may depend on the Holy Spirit to truly make us strong.

What are the issues of self-reliance that stand in your way of learning to truly trust Jesus to be your complete source in living the Crucified Life? What are the subtle displays of self-reliance that come your way that affects the flow of God's Holy Spirit in you?

The great mistake made by most of the Lord's people is in hoping to discover in themselves that which is to be found in Christ alone. —A.W. Pink

DAY SEVENTEEN: THE POWER OF SUFFERING

For it has been granted to you on behalf of Christ not only to believe on Him, but also to suffer for him... (Phil. 1:30)

Book Reading: Read Chapter Three—Christlikeness Includes Suffering

Scripture Focus: Christlikeness Includes Suffering (Phil. 3:7-10; Hebrews 2:10, 18)

Jesus faced suffering when He was tempted. We normally think of Jesus as breezing through His temptation episodes as though they had no effect upon Him. A careful reading of the temptation texts see angels having to come to minister to Jesus because of the intensity of the temptations that He faced. He suffered immensely through the things by which He was tempted and in a way that we have never had to face.

For most of us, this is a touchy area, as it raises the question of whether or not Jesus could have sinned. That conversation misses the point entirely. He did not sin, because He was already the spotless Son of God. He did not become the spotless Son of God because He did not sin. He was already the Spotless One. And indeed, it is this Spotless One who became sin, the consequence of temptation. This was the greater horror.

The Crucified Life recognises our own security over sin and temptation and demands that we live our lives over sin. It forces us to create a healthy holiness and to be steadfast in our resistance to the pull of the temptation to sin. Do you feel the dirtiness of sin when you fall?

Christ, because He was the only Man who never yielded to temptation, is also the only Man who knows to the full what temptation means. —C.S. Lewis

DAY EIGHTEEN: THE POWER OF SUFFERING

For it has been granted to you on behalf of Christ not only to believe on Him, but also to suffer for him... (Phil. 1:30)

Book Reading: Read Chapter Three—Incarnational Suffering
Scripture Focus: Incarnational Suffering (Luke 2:52; Phil. 2:5-8, Hebrews 10:32-9)

Here in the West, physical persecution is generally yet unknown, but there is no doubt that it shall come. Churches will be losing their properties; individual believers will be forced to give up their properties and rights. Some will face hardship, persecution, imprisonment and loss just as fellow believers elsewhere have had to endure and are enduring. We must not suppose that because we are in the 'free' West, that such things will not happen to us. It shall come upon the Western church as night follows day and the believers must be prepared.

Jesus grew up in a real world, and had to face real life challenges. He didn't have it any easier because He was the Child of God. He was called nasty names, called the product of sexual sin, a blasphemer, one who caroused with sinners, mad, demon possessed and the like.

It is only as we begin to live properly for Jesus that these things come to be said of us and of our personal faith. Peter encourages that when these things are said of us that we are to ensure that they are not true. The Crucified Life, lives out Christ in a real world before real people with opinions that carry real consequences. How are you living out the Crucified Life?

The supreme test of goodness is not in the greater but in the smaller incidents of our character and practice; not what we are when standing in the searchlight of public scrutiny, but when we reach the firelight flicker of our homes; not what we are when some clarion-call rings through the air, summoning us to fight for life and liberty, but our attitude when we are called to sentry-duty in the gray morning, when the watch-fire is burning low. It is impossible to be our best at the supreme moment if character is corroded and eaten into by daily inconsistency, unfaithfulness, and besetting sin. —F.B. Meyer.

DAY NINETEEN:
THE POWER OF SUFFERING

For it has been granted to you on behalf of Christ not only to believe on Him, but also to suffer for him... (Phil. 1:30)

Book Reading: Read Chapter Three—Modelling Suffering
Scripture Focus: Modelling Suffering (1 Peter 1:6, 1 Peter 2:19-21).

Consciousness of God in the face of suffering is among the greatest assets that anyone can have and hold on to. Peter repeats the Pauline theme that enduring the Crucified Life is best modelled with the understanding and security of the presence of the Lord.

Suffering always seems to assume that God is silent, or that God has left us to bear some test alone. But perhaps in the very place of suffering is the very place of the most intense embrace of God. Suffering does not and will never mean that God has left us. That happened once—at Calvary and is never to be repeated.

What suffering are you facing today? Where do you suppose God is in the violence of the pain that may be shaking you? Does it matter where He is in the face of your pain?

"We know that all things work together for good to them that love God" (Romans 8:28). The Christian does not merely hold this as a theory, but he knows it as a matter of fact. Everything has worked for good as yet; the poisonous drugs mixed in fit proportions have worked the cure; the sharp cuts of the lancet have cleansed out the proud flesh and facilitated the healing. Every event as yet has worked out the most divinely blessed results; and so, believing that God rules all, that He governs wisely, that He brings good out of evil, the believer's heart is assured, and he is enabled calmly to meet each trial as it comes. The believer can in the spirit of true resignation pray,

Send me what Thou wilt, my God, so long as it comes from Thee; never came there an ill portion from Thy table to any of Thy children. —C.H. Spurgeon

DAY TWENTY:
THE POWER OF SUFFERING

For it has been granted to you on behalf of Christ not only to believe on Him, but also to suffer for him... (Phil. 1:30)

Book Reading: Read Chapter Three—Suffering as Purification
Scripture Focus: Suffering as Purification (1 Peter 4:1; 1 Peter 5:10)

My spiritual discipler, Rev. Courtney Richards, has been very strong on this point. In a whole or total sense, through faith we come to belong to Jesus and yet, we must resist the anxiety to recoil into ourselves when we are forced to face the challenges of surrendering the parts of ourselves to Him—intentionally, deliberately, and decisively.

As we offer the various parts of ourselves, we soon begin to see the magnitude of the work that must be done as we are being pressed, again and again on the potter's wheel. God patiently, intentional and graciously purges us through a process that when He is done with us we become that display of His splendour.

In what areas has God been taking you over the Potter's wheel? Where do you think you are in the process of your purification? The Crucified Life assumes this as a necessity rather than an option. Can you share it with others?

Our vision is so limited we can hardly imagine a love that does not show itself in protection from suffering.... The love of God did not protect His own Son.... He will not necessarily protect us—not from anything it takes to make us like His Son. A lot of hammering and chiseling and purifying by fire will have to go into the process. —Elisabeth Elliot

DAY TWENTY-ONE:
THE POWER OF SUFFERING

For it has been granted to you on behalf of Christ not only to believe on Him, but also to suffer for him... (Phil. 1:30)

Book Reading: Read Chapter Three—Suffering as Paternal Disciplining

Scripture Focus: Suffering as Paternal Disciplining (Num. 12:14-16).

In a faithful relationship between a father and his child, that child is going to be bound to experience some of the consequences of his disobedience. While it does not cancel the relationship between father and child, the father is bound to teach that behaviour has consequences.

While the father may at times leave the child to the consequences of his behaviour, there can be no doubt regarding the father's own attitude to the wayward child. He loves that child, even though he has to face the consequences prescribed for waywardness. The father's intention is not to maim the child beyond recovery or to kill him, but rather his intention is to shepherd him back to his senses. In the story of the Lost Son in Luke 15, the text tells us how the young man made some choices, which led him to the very end of himself, until he came back to his senses.

The Crucified Life may see God in His role as father having to sternly and graciously allow us some measure of the consequences of our disobedience. Is there a particular way that God's hand may be heavy upon you in disciplinary care? What attitude are you displaying to Him and to that disciplinary care?

How can you balance discipline and love? Discipline is an expression of love... Rather than being something to balance with love, it is the deepest expression of love.
—Tedd Tripp

DAY TWENTY-TWO:
THE POWER OF SUFFERING

For it has been granted to you on behalf of Christ not only to believe on Him, but also to suffer for him... (Phil. 1:30)

Book Reading: Read Chapter Three—Paul's Thorn in the Flesh
Scripture Focus: Paul's Thorn in the Flesh (2 Cor. 12:7-10)

Paul explains that fourteen years ago, God allowed him into paradise or the third heaven and showed him some things there that no human lips can express. He says that God showed him such visions and revelations that would boggle the mind. Obviously, any believer would be excited by these things and probably would be disposed to feel particularly uniquely special at the privilege. It was indeed a unique privilege but to keep the apostle from making that experience the source of his faith in God, God allowed Satan to inflict some wound upon him.

Sometimes God takes pre-emptive action to save us from headed in the wrong direction, even if the action seems unpleasant in the moment. The purpose for Paul's thorn was that through it God would keep Paul from becoming conceited. For Paul the antidote for conceit was a thorn in the flesh. The Lord indeed knows how to deliver the righteous.

The Crucified Life recognises that God intervenes with some things that we might find unpleasant as a means to keep us from sin and from losing purpose. In what ways may God have given you a thorn to keep you from being proud or to keep you from anything else which may bring dishonour to His purpose in you?

The focus of health in the soul is humility, while the root of inward corruption is pride. In the spiritual life, nothing stands still. If we are not constantly growing downward into humility, we shall be steadily swelling up and running to seed under the influence of pride. —J.I. Packer

DAY TWENTY-THREE:
THE POWER OF SUFFERING

For it has been granted to you on behalf of Christ not only to believe on Him, but also to suffer for him... (Phil. 1:30)

Book Reading: Read Chapter Three—Pilgrimage as Suffering
Scripture Focus: Pilgrimage as Suffering (Phil. 3: 20; 1 Peter 1:17; 1 Peter 2:11)

If more Christians were living as strangers and pilgrims in the land rather than as citizens at ease in the land, then the sharpness of the suffering that they would have to face would be more telling. Christian suffering on a whole is not as obvious because in many instances, Christianity has been compromised by believers who have not made the distinction in their lives of being in the world, and not of the world, of living by the Spirit and not by the flesh and knowing the wiles of the devil and not giving him a foothold.

Ours is a countercultural faith. We pray, "Let your Kingdom come" for that very reason. We belong elsewhere, we want the features of our actual home to become the features here, and the powers that be are not giving up without their fiercest fight. Each one of us is placed strategically to make that happen.

We must repudiate our confused loyalties and concerns for the passing world and put aside our misguided efforts to change culture externally. To allow our thoughts, plans, time, money, and energy to be spent trying to make a superficially Christian (world), or to put a veneer of morality over the world, is to distort the gospel, misconstrue our divine calling, and squander our God-given resources. We must not weaken our spiritual mission, obscure our

priority of proclaiming the gospel of salvation, or become confused about our spiritual citizenship, loyalties and obligations. We are to change society, but by faithfully proclaiming the gospel, which changes lives on the inside.
—John McArthur.

DAY TWENTY-FOUR:
THE POWER OF SUFFERING

For it has been granted to you on behalf of Christ not only to believe on Him, but also to suffer for him... (Phil. 1:30)

Book Reading: Read Chapter three—Learning hard Lessons
Scripture Focus: Learning Hard Lessons (Gen. 16:7-9)

The Crucified Life is also manifest when God wants us to learn something that we have difficulty learning. Sometimes the process of learning may be tedious, and we get hard knocks along the way. He is not intending to destroy us in the process. His intention is that we might be restored and that we might function at a higher purposive level.

So God chose to send Hagar back into the lap of a difficult situation. And sometimes even when we think that our circumstances are undeserved, it may be that God is in a process of making the character of Christ, as unique as it may be to us individually, remain qualitatively excellent in us.

What hard situation do you think that God is putting you back into on account of the fact that He is still working out some things in you as you commit to live out the Crucified Life...a difficult marriage? A church you don't want to be at? A work place or a boss that is giving you all the trouble you could ask for? Sickness?

God doesn't give you the people you want, He gives you the people you need to help you, to hurt you, to leave you, to love you and to make you the person you were meant to be. —Unknown

DAY TWENTY-FIVE: THE POWER OF SUFFERING

For it has been granted to you on behalf of Christ not only to believe on Him, but also to suffer for him... (Phil. 1:30)

Book Reading: Read Chapter Three—the Divine Boast
Scripture Focus: The Divine Boast and Suffering (Job 2:7, 19:17-20, Job 2:7,8, 7:4, 5, 30:10, 17, 30)

Job encountered this, and believers throughout the centuries have undergone this type of trial. The scriptures explain that the believer is God's workmanship whom God puts on display to the universe from time to time (Eph. 2:9ff). In the display of His workmanship, the accuser will come before God to seek to separate God from that which is His. This was the attempt that he made against Job. He told God that Job was only serving Him for what he could get. God was confident that such was not the case and so Job was put through amazing pain and suffering.

God says to Satan, "Have you seen my servant _____ [put your name here]." What do you think would happen? The Crucified Life means that God is willing to call your name to the enemy. God has full confidence in who you are, not because of your opinion of yourself, but because of His attitude towards and outlook concerning you.

God is confident of who you are. He is confident of how you are maturing in Him. He is pleased at your progress in Him. He is sure that you will stand up for Him showing you off in the spirit realm. How do you feel?

The LORD your God is with you, the Mighty Warrior who saves. He will take great delight in you; in his love he will no longer rebuke you, but will rejoice over you with singing. (Zeph. 3:17)

DAY TWENTY-SIX:
THE POWER OF SUFFERING

For it has been granted to you on behalf of Christ not only to believe on Him, but also to suffer for him... (Phil. 1:30)

Book Reading: Read Chapter three—Suffering and the glory of God
Scripture Focus: Suffering and the glory of God (John 9:1-3)

Think of Nick Vujicic, the Australian, born without hands or legs and who has been making great strides for the kingdom of God. Nick Vujicic has made this astounding point. "If God can use a man without arms and legs to be His hands and feet, then He will certainly use any willing heart!"

Or think of the great Christian artiste Joni Eareckson-Tada who as a result of a diving accident was left a quadriplegic in a wheelchair who in her work *The God I Love* says "...we will stand amazed to see the topside of the tapestry and how God beautifully embroidered each circumstance into a pattern for our good and His glory." In the same work she says, "Sometimes God allows what he hates to accomplish what he loves."

Can you truly say with Paul that, we know that all things work together for good... All things?

He cleansed suffering! It was no longer a sign of our being caught in the wheel of existence, as Buddha suggests; no longer the result of our evil deeds of a previous birth, as our Hindu friends tell us; no longer the sign of the displeasure of God, as many of all ages and of all religions have suggested; no longer something to be stoically and doggedly borne. It is more than that. Suffering is the gift of God. —E. Stanley Jones

DAY TWENTY- SEVEN:
THE POSITIONAL BLESSINGS OF
JESUS' CRUCIFIXION

But we see Jesus, who was made a little lower than the angels, now crowned with glory and honour, because he suffered death, so that by the grace of God He might taste death for everyone (Heb. 2:9)

Book Reading: Read Chapter Four—Tasting of Death for Everyone

Scripture Focus: Tasting of Death for Everyone (Hebrews 2:9)

Among the strongest theological themes of the scriptures is the message that the wages of sin is death. From Adam in Genesis 2 and to those described as dogs in Revelation 22, the sentence is the same. Death and separation from God are the natural lot of all men. Life then is impossible for men who constantly live in sin and who carry its sentence upon their shoulders.

Living The Crucified Life is lifting the burden of being under the weight of sin. It is the very point that Paul makes. Dead to sin, means that the believer no longer lives under the penalty of Sin.

Do you fully understand this true fact, that Jesus' death means your death to sin in every way?

[Jesus] saves His people from their sins. This is His special office. He saves them from the guilt of sin, by washing them in His own atoning blood. He saves them from the dominion of sin, by putting in their hearts the sanctifying Spirit. He saves them from the presence of sin, when He takes them out of this world to rest with Him. He will save

them from all the consequences of sin, when He shall give them a glorious body at the last day. Blessed and holy are Christ's people! From sorrow, cross, and conflict they are not saved. But they are saved from sin for evermore.
—J.C. Ryle

DAY TWENTY-EIGHT:
THE POSITIONAL BLESSINGS OF
JESUS' CRUCIFIXION

Book Reading: Read Chapter Four—His Death breaks the Power of Devil (Hebrews 2:14, 15)
Scripture Focus: His Death breaks the Power of Devil (Hebrews 2:14, 15)

There is no fear of death lurking in the heart of the believer. Every believer knows that the sting of death has been removed and its horror taken away. Indeed, the believer has so thoroughly triumph over death that the believer who has died physically is described as fallen asleep in the Lord (1 Cor. 15: 20, 1 Thes 4: 14). It is a most telling description of the powerlessness of the hold of death upon the already crucified believer. Death cannot kill that which is already crucified.

The dividing walls have been removed. Jesus secured our peace. God's will is that the enmity that existed between the earth and the throne-room would cease. In the death of Jesus He tore down the middle wall of partition which separated people from each other and which separated God from the people.

Are you free to relate to God and others the way God wants you to because of your Crucified Life?

In God's case, if He had said in the infinite sovereignty of His absolute will, 'I will have no substitute, but each man shall suffer for himself, he who sinneth shall die,' none could have murmured. It was grace, and only grace which led the divine mind to say, "I will accept a substitute. There shall be a vicarious suffering; and My vengeance

shall be content, and My mercy shall be gratified.
—Charles Spurgeon

DAY TWENTY-NINE:
THE POSITIONAL BLESSINGS OF
JESUS' CRUCIFIXION

Eternal Redemption (Hebrews 9:12)

Book Reading: Read Chapter Four—A Clean Conscience
Scripture Focus: A Cleansed Consciences (Hebrews 9:14)

The Crucified Life includes a new conscience –a conscience bathed in the blood of Jesus. The Bible describes several possible characteristics of the conscience: a pure conscience (1 Tim. 3:9, 2 Tim. 1:3), the good conscience (Acts 23:1,1 Tim. 1:5,19; Heb. 13:8, 1 Pet. 3:16, 21), the conscience void of offence or a clear conscience (Acts 24:16, 1 Cor. 4:4), the conscience which bears witness or a confirming conscience (Rom. 2:15, 9: 1, 2 Cor. 1:12), a weak and defiled conscience (1 Cor. 8: 7-10), A seared conscience (1 Tim. 4:2) and an evil conscience (Heb. 10:22)

The conscience regenerated by the Holy Spirit is used by the Crucified Life in a way that guides conduct as led by the Holy Spirit. A conscience so yielded to the Holy Spirit is very important to guide Christian living.

Have we properly given our consciences fully over to the Holy Spirit for training and correction? Are there aspects of conscience still governed by the permissible in the world or in the tug of the flesh which seek to justify its desires?

Conscience is to the soul what pain is to the body. We would like to avoid pain as much as possible, but at the same time we recognize that pain is a gift from God. If you didn't have pain, you would destroy yourself. Pain is critical to physical preservation. And so the conscience is critical to spiritual preservation. —John MacArthur

DAY THIRTY:
THE POSITIONAL BLESSINGS OF
JESUS' CRUCIFIXION

Book Reading: Read Chapter Four—The Sacrifice of Himself
does away with Sin
Scripture Focus: The Sacrifice of Himself does away with Sin
(Heb. 9:26, 28)

When Jesus went to the cross and He sacrificed Himself, He settled every question of sin, so that those who live in Him would be empowered to live beyond acts of the sin nature, beyond the deception of the world and beyond the allure of false spirits.

In the cross, every sin is accounted for and taken away. The Crucified Life is a call to live in the truth of this reality. In His death, there is no need for a repeat performance. It was an all-sufficient, efficacious and decisive act. In this death, no further sacrifice is necessary.

Do we still feel we must continue to hold on to our sins for fear that we might not appear remorseful enough? While there must be godly sorrow over sin, the Crucified Life is a reminder that it is He, not us who pays for them. We must not wallow in self-pity.

Self-pity sounds self-sacrificing. The reason self-pity does not look like pride is that it appears to be so needy. But the need arises from a wounded ego. It doesn't come from a sense of unworthiness, but from a sense of unrecognized worthiness. It is the response of un-applauded pride. Christian Hedonism severs the root of self-pity. People don't feel self-pity when suffering is accepted for the sake of joy. —John Piper

DAY THIRTY-ONE:
THE POSITIONAL BLESSINGS OF
JESUS' CRUCIFIXION

Perfection Forever for those Being made Holy (Hebrews 10:15)

Book Reading: Read Chapter Four—Confidence
Scripture Focus: Confidence (Hebrews 10:19, 20)

What a privilege it is to live in the confidence of the Crucified Life. Those who have come to the cross have already been made holy and have been perfected in Christ by that cross. This is a most appealing spiritual reality. This is not the offer of sinless perfection in this body, but rather the fact that God sees us as complete in Christ Jesus (Col. 2:10).

We then can enter the Throne Room with confidence, not "storm the Throne of Grace" as some are wont to do, but know that we can enter there with confidence, without having to look over our shoulders because of failures or mistakes or thinking that God wears an eternal frown.

How confident do you feel when you enter the Throne Room of God? What keeps you there as you stand? What makes you want to leave? How do you resolve that conflict, if any exist?

Uncertainty as to our relationship with God is one of the most enfeebling and dispiriting of things. It makes a man heartless. It takes the pith out of him. He cannot fight; he cannot run. He is easily dismayed and gives way. He can do nothing for God. But when we know that we are of God, we are vigorous, brave, invincible. There is no more quickening truth than this of assurance. —Horatius Bona

DAY THIRTY-TWO: CRUCIFIXION AND THE NEW CREATION

Therefore, if anyone is in Christ, he is a new creation; the old has gone, the new has come! (2 Cor. 5:17)

Book Reading: Read Chapter Five —The New Space
Scripture Focus: The New Space (1 Cor. 15:45, 2 Cor. 4: 6)

The Crucified Life removes us from taking our direction from the natural realm and places us in the realm of the Spirit. This is a totally different place from which to live now. Here we become God's new creation, children of the new (last) Adam living in a new light.

Everything becomes new for us in respect to our point of reference for life and meaning. We now live by faith and not by sight (2 Cor. 5:7). It is God's divine power which now gives us everything that we need for life and for godliness (2 Peter 1:3). We now live in that light, not of the old Sun, but now under the Son of righteousness. We are no longer aligned to the old Adam who lives in the corruption of fallenness, but in the power of an endless life in Christ Jesus.

How do you navigate the tension of living physically in this world, but appreciating the power of the new dynamic of living from the point of view of the new creation, under the Last Adam and in a new light?

God became man to turn creatures into sons: not simply to produce better men of the old kind but to produce a new kind of man. —C.S. Lewis

DAY THIRTY-THREE: CRUCIFIXION AND THE NEW CREATION

Therefore, if anyone is in Christ, he is a new creation; the old has gone, the new has come! (2 Cor.5:17)

Book Reading: Read Chapter Five—The New Space
Scripture Focus: The New Space continued (Hebrews 3:7, 8, 12:18-24, Gal. 5:6)

The Crucified Life is a lifestyle no longer bound by the old order of worship either. In this new space, a new day has been given called "Today" a new law given, not six hundred an thirteen parts, but one, faith expressing itself in love and a new worship experience, not one centred around fear and fright but rather acceptance and affirmation.

Here the believer begins to see himself as he really is - beyond the power and reach of the enemy, more than a conqueror, strengthened by Christ through the power of the Holy Spirit.

What does it mean to you to be a new creation in Christ Jesus in light of these new realities?

Nothing paralyzes our lives like the attitude that things can never change. We need to remind ourselves that God can change things. Outlook determines outcome. If we see only the problems, we will be defeated; but if we see the possibilities in the problems, we can have victory.
—Warren Wiersbe

DAY THIRTY-FOUR:
THE POWER OF THE WILL

For if you live according to the sinful nature, you will die; but if by the Sprit you put to death the misdeeds of the body you will live (Rom. 8:13).

Book Reading: Read Chapter Six—The Power of the Will
Scripture Focus: Take my will (John 5:19)

There is nothing so powerful in God's hand as a surrendered will. A surrendered will gives up the right to oneself and acquiesces to the higher call. It renounces the right to end up destroyed and embraces the way to life—true life

For many, this is perhaps among the most painful of experiences—surrendering the will. This is because the most important of our possessions is our will. Take away my will and there is nothing left of me—my freedoms, my hopes, my dreams and yet this is the request of the Crucified life—to surrender the will to a sovereign loving God.

Take my will and make it Thine it shall be no longer mine.
Take my heart it is thine own; it shall be thy royal throne.
Take my love, my Lord I pour at your feet its treasure store.
Take myself and I will be ever, only all for thee,
Take myself and I will be ever, only all for thee.
Here am I, All of me.
Take my life, It's all for thee.
—Christopher Tomlin/Louie Giglio

Above all else, we must learn how to bring our wills into submission and obedience to the will of God, on a practical, daily, hour-by-hour basis. —Jerry Bridges

DAY THIRTY-FIVE:
CRUCIFYING THE FLESH

Put to death, therefore, whatever belongs to your sinful nature: sexual immorality, impurity, lust, evil desires and greed, which is idolatry (Col. 3:5)

Book Reading: Read Chapter seven—Crucifying the Flesh
Scripture Focus: The Flesh—Romans 8:5-13

Paul explains that those who live by the sin nature have their minds set on what the sinful nature wants, they cannot please God and will die because the sinful mind is death and it is hostile to God. Retaining the sinful nature is like retaining old clothes from the Old Order of things. What the Crucified Life requires is a life submitted to the will of God where every time the sin nature fights back it is laid aside as though it were some old clothes no longer being worn.

This is to be replaced with the new clothes that God has given us to wear. We are to clothe ourselves firstly with humility. When the sin nature meets humility there us the immediate reminder that the strength of the Crucified Life lies not in itself, but the God who gives news clothes of righteousness.

How are you dealing with the pull of the sinful nature in your space?

I could fight the devil; I could overcome every sin that ever tempted me, if it were not that I had an enemy within. Those Diabolians within do more service to Satan than all the Diabolians without. As Bunyan says in his Holy War, the enemy tried to get some of his friends within the City of Mansoul, and he found his darlings inside the walls did him far more good than all those without. Ah! Christians, thou couldst laugh at thine enemy, if thou hadst not thine evil heart within; but remember, thine heart keeps the keys, because out of it are the issues of life. And sin is there. The worst thing thou has to fear is the treachery of thine own heart. —C.H. Spurgeon

DAY THIRTY-SIX:
CRUCIFYING THE WORLD

May I never boast except in the cross of our Lord Jesus Christ through which the world has been crucified to me and I to the world (Gal. 6:14)

Book Reading: Read Chapter Eight—Crucifying the World
Scripture Focus: Fighting Worldliness (Romans 1:28-32)

Here are some truths about the world: These are some of the truths that the scriptures record about the world:

- The world does not know the Spirit, Jesus, the Father, nor the believers (John 1:10, 14:17, 17:25; 1 John 3:1)
- The kingdom of Jesus does not belong to this world (John 18:36)
- In a day to come, Jesus will judge the world (Acts 17:31)
- Whoever is a friend of the world is an enemy of God (James 4:4)
- The world hates the believers (John 15:18, 17:14; 1 John 3:13)
- The whole world is under the control of the evil one (1 John 5:19; John 12:31, 14:30, 16:11; 2 Cor. 4:4)

The Crucified Life is fully aware of the subtle pull of the world, and appreciates the structure in which it functions. The Crucified Life sees the intent of the world for what it simply is—to undermine the God of the universe and His will.

Living the Crucified Life in such a space requires double vigilance. How attentive are we in our vigilance against worldliness?

Can you truly say, that you have so far taken the everlasting enjoyment of God for your happiness, that it has the most of your heart, of your love, desire, and care; and that you are resolved, by the strength of Divine grace, to let go all that you have in the world, rather than hazard it; and that it is your daily, and your principal business to seek it? Can you truly say, that though you have your failings and sins, yet your main care, and the bent of your whole life, is to please God, and to enjoy him forever; and that you give the world God's leavings, as it were, and not God the world's leavings; and that your worldly business is but as a traveller's seeking for provision in his journey, and heaven is the place that you take for your home? —Richard Baxter

DAY THIRTY-SEVEN:
VICTORY OVER LEGALISM
AND THE LAW

He forgave us all our sins, having cancelled the written code, with its regulations that was against us and that stood opposed to us; he took it away nailing it to the cross (Col. 2:13, 14).

Book Reading: Read Chapter Nine—Victory over Legalism and the Law
Scripture Focus: Legalism (Romans 7:4-14, Gal. 2:16, Gal. 3:10)

O ne of the most important things that the Crucified Life re- cognises is that no amount of goodness will be good enough to live the way God wants. In fact the most remarkable legal system (the Law given at Mount Sinai) could not impart life, and the Bible teaches that anyone who tries to be made right with God by observing that legal system remains under a curse.

The Crucified Life also means that we cannot depend on any prop to live the way God wants us to live. It must be a total faith walk. It is so serious that trying to obey the Law to be made right with God places such a person at enmity with God. This does not mean that the Law is not good, but simply that its purpose is not served in that sense. As good as it is, that which is good ended up bringing death

Are there some good things that we might be holding on to make us right with God outside of the life surrendered totally and completely to Him? Is it the Christ life which is flowing through you through faith?

Faith is rest, not toil. It is the giving up all the former weary efforts to do or feel something good, in order to in-

duce God to love and pardon; and the calm reception of the truth so long rejected, that God is not waiting for any such inducements, but loves and pardons of His own goodwill, and is showing that goodwill to any sinner who will come to Him on such a footing, casting away his own poor performances or goodnesses, and relying implicitly upon the free love of Him who so loved the world that He gave His only begotten Son. —Horatius Bonar

DAY THIRTY-EIGHT:
VICTORY OVER POWERS AND AUTHORITIES

And having disarmed the powers and authorities he made a public spectacle of them, triumphing over them by the cross (Col. 2:15).

Book Reading: Read Chapter Ten—Victory over Powers and Authorities

Scripture Focus: Fighting principalities and Powers (Eph. 6:10-20)

The demonic world is real. The scriptures describe the work of Satan and demons in several ways. The scriptures include the following verses:

- Jesus describes Satan as coming to steal, to kill and to destroy (John 10:10).
- Satan masquerades as an angel of light seeking to deceive people (2 Cor. 11:14).
- The Devil traps, captures and enslaves people to do his will (2 Tim. 2:26).
- Satan prowls around like a roaring lion seeking to devour whom he may (2 Pet. 5:8).
- Demons possess people causing them to become physically sick, emotionally sick and spiritually sick (Matt. 4:24).

The Crucified Life recognises that it is standing in Christ which secures victory over the enemy. It is submitting to God which enables the believer to effectively resist. It is in this sense that demons do not have to be "cast out" of the believer, but by which the enemy runs from the believer.

What weapons have you been using in your fight against principalities and powers arrayed against you as a child of God? Can you relate this to the Crucified Life?

There are two equal and opposite errors into which our race can fall about the devils. One is to disbelieve in their existence. The other is to believe, and to feel an excessive and unhealthy interest in them. They themselves are equally pleased by both errors, and hail a materialist and a magician with the same delight. —C.S. Lewis

DAY THIRTY NINE:
SAMSON AND THE CRUCIFIED LIFE

And what more shall I say? I do not have time to tell about Gideon, Barak, Samson,... who through faith conquered kingdoms, administered justice, and gained what was promised;... (Heb. 11:32-33)

Book Reading: Chapter Eleven—Samson and the Crucified Life

Samson displayed serious character flaws including impetuosity, invincibility, arrogance, sexual immorality and anger. And yet, he was a man used by God both before the Holy Spirit left him, and then when again his hair began to grow again. What could have happened in such a life?

It was a failure not to depend on God in all that he was in spite of the great gifts he had. The gift is always greater than the man. The "anointing" from God is no proof of spiritual integrity in the man. There has to be that willingness to allow the formation of God's character in the Crucified Life. There is a risk which leads to one becoming victim of one's "success"

How successfully are you living out the Crucified Life? What are your strong areas and how might you be vulnerable because of the areas of your success?

The Christian often tries to forget his weakness; God wants us to remember it, to feel it deeply. The Christian wants to conquer his weakness and to be freed from it; God wants us to rest and even rejoice in it. The Christian mourns over his weakness; Christ teaches His servant to say, 'I take pleasure in infirmities. Most gladly... will I... glory in my infirmities' (2 Cor. 12:9). The Christian thinks his weaknesses are his greatest hindrance in the life and service of God; God tells us that it is the secret of strength and success. It is our weakness, heartily accepted and continually realized, that gives our claim and access to the strength of Him who has said, 'My strength is made perfect in weakness.' —Andrew Murray

DAY FORTY:
THE LORD'S TABLE

For whenever you eat this bread and drink this cup you proclaim the Lord's death until he comes (1 Cor. 11:26)

Book Reading: Chapter Thirteen—The Lord's Table

The Lord's Table is at once, a memorial, a present reality and blessed hope. In this one act, time collapses and transfers us outside of the physical limitations of time and space. In three hours Jesus bore hell and defeated every enemy which stood against the believer. It is in the collapse of time that we see eternity. The Crucified Life does a similar thing. It teaches us to live our lives from the perspective of eternity, not from the time and space dimensions.

This new blood covenant is the ultimate covenant of love and life where being with God means loving and serving God, not gratifying ourselves, it means sharing in His glory because we are royalty with all of the privileges and benefits of that position. It is here that we see Jesus finally, the One who retains humanness in the form of God. It is Him supernaturally transforming humanness into what being sons of God should have been in the first place.

When you come to the Table and break the Bread and take the Cup, what does it mean to you?

The New Covenant is the bond between God and man, established by the sacrificial death of Jesus Christ, under which all who have been effectively called to God in all ages have been formed into the one body of Christ in New Testament times, in order to come under His law during this age and to remain under His authority forever. —Tom Wells

ABOUT THE AUTHOR

Since installation as Pastor at Maverley Gospel Hall in October 2002, the Lord has continued to use Pastor Napoleon St. Patrick Black both locally and overseas. He has shared the gospel across the length and breadth of Jamaica, several Caribbean nations, in the United States and in South Africa.

Pastor Black is founder of the para-church ministry, Pastors According to His Heart (PATHH), a support ministry to pastors and their families. He has served on several government and para-church boards as well. He has been sharing on his denomination's radio programme "Look at Life" for just about 20 years and has been serving the Love 101 radio programme "To Have and to Hold" since 2015.

Pastor Black grew up in the picturesque Holland Village in St. Elizabeth, Jamaica. His love for the Lord soon grew out of his mother's passion for spiritual things and her insisting that days would end with her children on their knees before the Lord repeating both the Lord's Prayer and the Twenty Third Psalm.

This passion for the Lord grew in Pastor Black as he left for secondary education to the inimitable Munro College at the top of the scenic Santa Cruz Mountains. Here his spiritual formation continued as his calling to the Lord was finally and firmly established there and his spiritual gifts began to manifest.

After school, he found employment in banking and within seven years, felt called to full time ministry. With his young family, he began serving the Lord, both at Grace Gospel Chapel and Brucefield Gospel Chapel in St. Elizabeth, Jamaica. The Lord used him to great effect in helping to strengthen the believers and to serve those communities.

In 1997, the Lord led Pastor Black to formal training at the Jamaica Theological Seminary. There he continued to make his mark as a leader, serving both as Resident Advisor and President of the Student Council. There he continued on the path of servant leader.

Pastor Black, together with his wife Aneita, (a primary school teacher), are parents to two grown children and two grandchildren.

www.ingramcontent.com/pod-product-compliance
Lightning Source LLC
LaVergne TN
LVHW011222080426
835509LV00005B/261